EDITED BY PETER BAXTER

STERNBERG

1980
BFI Publishing

Published by the British Film Institute
127 Charing Cross Road
London WC2H 0EA

Cover design: John Gibbs

ISBN 0 85170 098 5 (hardback)
    0 85170 099 3 (paperback)

Set and printed by Tonbridge Printers Ltd
Shipbourne Road, Tonbridge, Kent

Contents

PETER BAXTER

Introduction

The human eye, with a lateral field of vision of approximately 180°, has an angle of sharp focus at the centre of that field of only 3°; away from that focal centre, toward the periphery of the field, shape and colour decreasingly stimulate the optic nerve, which eventually at the edge of perception responds only to motion. When we look into the night sky certain dim stars disappear as we turn our eyes toward where we sensed their presence; their twinkling attracted our attention, but they are not sufficiently bright to retain it. Recent materialist film study, quite properly focused on problems of ideology, culture, and the film institution, senses a presence beckoning for its attention, one that seems to vanish as the eye is shifted toward it. This presence is the artist, the film author, that shimmering star whose position seems constant in our firmament, but whose actuality dissolves under scrutiny, becoming an ideological construction, a projected fantasy, an effect of texts — filmic and printed, artistic and critical — circulating in society, producing and maintaining a certain orientation of the individual subject within the social formation.

Obviously this effect is not altogether different from that of religion, and it has recently been pointed out once more that much of what passes for film criticism participates directly in authorial cultism.[1] This having been said, however, it still seems necessary to recognise that even at its most journalistically idolatrous, commentary on the movies is neverthe-less a material constituent of cultural production, and that if its mode of operation is to crystallise an imaginary presence around a name, that name is appropriated to ideology from its bearer in material production, from the actor, from the director, from the real person to whom it belongs, from the real situation in which s/he lives. Ideological structures are not entirely illusory: they take off, as it were, from the material conditions of production in order to effect an imaginary distortion of those conditions. In the case of authorial cultism, it seems that what occurs is a deflection of awareness from the real presence of a being engaged in material production at a certain moment in history, whose options for activity are determined by his/her position in the relations of production; a deflection toward the authorial presence, toward the unreality of inspired expression.

In order to grasp the reality of the director's presence in dominant cinema, it is necessary to grasp the reality of commodity production, a

1

reality that began to set the terms of cultural production long before the cinema was invented. The case of Alexandre Dumas *père* is exemplary of the historical specificity of artistic activity:

> In a court action it is proved that Dumas publishes more under his own name than he could write even if he were to work day and night without a break. In fact, he employs seventy-three collaborators. . . . Literary work now becomes a 'commodity' in the fullest sense of the word; it has its price tariff, is produced according to a pattern and delivered on a day fixed in advance. It is a commercial article for which one pays the price it is worth — the price it returns.[2]

Both Dumas the entrepreneur, and the employees who wrote as 'Dumas' are avatars of the age of emergent capitalism, the reality a law suit discovers behind the name on the title page.

Although we are directed away from the material conditions of production, and toward the institutional, imaginary relationship of reciprocal subjectivities and artistic expression, the means of deflection is in itself real and material, a part of the apparatus maintaining the social formation, and in the specificity of its operation it is of course determined by the historical moment of its functioning. When, for instance, *The Blue Angel* was released in London and New York the reviews of the film clearly structured its discourse in terms of the metropolitan cultural dominance of bourgeois theatre and its received mode of conceptualisation: the authorial subject they inscribe is predicated on Jannings the star-performer, rather than on Sternberg the absent director. 'Emil Jannings' performance . . . is marvellous', says the reviewer of *The Spectator*. 'Certainly he should help to develop the talking picture to at least a stage of adolescence.'[3] So far as the reviewers see him, Jannings stands centre-stage, so to speak, and their attention is rivetted upon his performance: the reviewer for *Punch* claims that he was 'filled by a real pity and horror for the tragedy'[4] because of Emil Jannings' playing of the part, and in *The New Statesman*, Michael Sadleir declares, 'Emil Jannings, the finest film-actor in Europe and America, has achieved a great tragic performance as the child-like, unworldly Professor Immanuel Rath. . . . the terrible story of Rath's slow degradation and final collapse into apathetic squalor, madness and death has a power which holds a huge audience motionless and silent . . . the story and the conflicting characterization are *acted*, and acted magnificently.'[5]

In America, the same occurred; *The Commonweal*, 31 December 1930:

> It is only the work of Jannings that deserves comment for its own sake. Speech helps, if anything, his mastery of screen technique. He is an artist of detail down to the least motion of his hands. When, for comedy, he repeats a certain scene, such as the morning opening of his

classes, he is careful to give just the right bit of variety and change. . . . In the tragedy which follows his marriage . . . he reaches rare heights of tragedy. It is good to know that he can now be numbered among the few great artists of the talking screen.[6]

These quotations of course exemplify a critical text which is only apparently different, at the surface level, from that which hails Josef von Sternberg as its subject. On this superficial level, the installation of 'Jannings' instead of 'Sternberg' as the creative actor/author of the film is self-evidently influenced by the relationship of these reviewers to the stage. As Richard Demarcy notes in *Eléments d'une sociologie du spectacle:* 'the process of identification is yet more complex because of the place given to the artist in our society, a place culminating in the notion of the star or the idol. . . . The bourgeois mode of reception of the theatre very often consists, as has been previously noted, of going to see the actor, his prowess, his performance.'[7]

The production of film, the production of the star, the production of the film-author are all aspects of an ultimately indivisible, material process; star and author are produced in the vast and fluid journalistic-cum-critical discourse that sweeps through the apparatus of the cinema like the tide through a coral reef. The question 'Who is speaking?' is important to anyone involved with a discourse that cannot be validated on the basis of immediate experience, and is therefore especially important in relation to fictional discourse. In the transformation of the productive apparatus of the American cinema into an industrial mode, there began the action of answering the question by foreclosing it at the ideological level of expressive communication. As early as 1930, it was widely accepted that 'when we see and hear a film, or rather when we *accept* a film, we are conscious of something beyond its theme and technical expression. We become aware of the director.'[8]

It was of course lamented during Sternberg's career, as often since, that under the conditions of 'big business' it was virtually impossible for the director really to assume the kind of control over his work exercised by an independent artist, and that the compromise (as Curtis Harrington called it[9]) by which the integrity of creativity subordinated itself to the tyranny of commerce was the reason that so little of what even Sternberg turned out was of certain, lasting value. Nevertheless, from relatively early on, certain directors — Vidor, Ingram, Cruze, for example — were recognised as having the superior strength which enabled them partially to overcome the circumstances within which they worked, and to make films of a notably personal character. For *The New York Times*, André Sennwald wrote: 'It requires no more than the fingers of one hand to itemize the Hollywood directors whose signatures are inscribed plainly and individually in their work. Mr. von Sternberg is one of them.'[10]

3

Sternberg is an exception, a true individual whose work is an expression of the difference of his being: 'his work is frequently hysterical, confused and incoherent. It screams with passion and shouts its intentions in crimson headlines. But as long ago as *The Salvation Hunters* he was doing things with a camera that nobody had ever done before, and he was demonstrating that for all his inarticulate frenzies he possesses the authentic seeds of cinematic greatness.'[11] Sennwald conforms to a notion of eccentricity tormenting the artist and isolating him — incoherent and inarticulate — from society. In later commentary this romantic notion is overtaken by a strain of commentary influenced by vulgar psychoanalysis, and having the same function of setting the artist apart, even if it refrains from talking about mysterious 'seeds of cinematic greatness', preferring to speculate on the subject's infantile experiences (see Marcel Oms' essay below).

It would by no means be correct to imply that this general inclusion of Sternberg among an elite of directors meant general agreement on the value of his work. That is not the point of what this inclusion intends. Rotha wrote of Sternberg's first film as director, *The Salvation Hunters:* 'it seems that if one makes a picture so dreary, so dull, and so depressing that it defeats criticism, then one will be hailed as a genius.'[12] The point is this hailing, this particular activity of producing the author-subject, whose purpose in the ideologised relations of production of society is to stand as a point of origin, and a point of authority, outside the laws of film-making, because the source of Law itself.[13]

This process was not confined to Anglo-American commentary, as the quotations I have chosen might suggest.

A dispatch from Paris in *The New York Times* of 20 April 1930 relates that two films, *Underworld* and *The Docks of New York*, had been playing to full houses for months on end, and appealing to both the mass cinema audience and the intelligentsia (see below for Morris Gilbert's report, 'Paris Cinema Chatter'). The dispatch does not mention that the director of these two films was Josef von Sternberg. He would not be left in such circumstances; our culture abhors anonymity as nature abhors a vacuum.

Louis Chavance's article here translated as 'The Case of Josef von Sternberg' substantiates the newspaper report of Parisian acclaim for Sternberg's films; in so doing, it firmly aligns itself within the critical practice of reading through a film its original source in the artist. The case of Josef von Sternberg is the mystery (and that is Chavance's word) of how works of erratically various worth could emanate from the genius of one man. More precisely, it is a case of establishing an identity — a subject — on the evidence of a number of contradictory statements, *the* identity that the films truly express. Chavance like many of Sternberg's commentators (cf. Rudolf Arnheim's essay) includes a brief biography of Sternberg (omitted from this translation), a gesture which lays the factitious foundations on which the subject will be erected. But Chavance calls Sternberg 'un grand anarchiste' and states that he cannot be grasped on the basis of his beliefs, that the channels of his thought cannot be charted, that he exceeds understanding.

In Italy during the thirties the same image of Sternberg was being produced. Sternberg was 'a fitful artist, it is true, tormented, given to excess, not immune to literary intoxication', wrote Ettore M. Margadonna, in 'Errori di Sternberg.'[14] Film direction, according to Margadonna, is not direction in the strict sense of the word, but 'autonomous artistic invention'.[15] Margadonna's problem is to stabilise the inventive subject responsible for all these films with their manifold contradictions.

Margadonna brings to bear on the problem of constituting an integral artist from the fragments of a work of art the myth of Pygmalion, and in so doing, in pointing out a Sternberg making errors in judgment, being swayed by passion, he poses a subject all the more credible in its conformity to certain bourgeois criteria for artist-hood. For *The Blue Angel*, Sternberg was fortunate enough to have found Dietrich, 'that is, a docile creature, easily moulded and influenced by a director capable of working on a woman as on a mass of clay.' That situation was perfect for a film which was a serious attempt to 'say something'; but following it, whether because he was 'inebriated with inspiration', or 'blinded by passion', instead of 'following his inspiration' he 'committed one of the most banal errors that are committed in the cinema: he did not search for new actors and actresses suited to his films, but searched for subjects suited to his actress.' The contradictions displayed by the films result from the errors of the artist, themselves the result of his genius, the eccentricity of which is distinguished by sexual appetite and sensual weakness.

What Margadonna deplored, Rudolph Arnheim interpreted as the increasing perfection of Sternberg's artistic control over an actress whom he also described as 'an extremely malleable woman'. Nevertheless, the superficiality of American culture, which for Arnheim is the product of a decay of values in the industrial age, leads to the very opposite of real art: 'the substitution of the most brazenly superficial gesture for real feelings.' And in this sense, Sternberg is prevented from joining the great master whom Arnheim reveres; that is, Sternberg is denied by Arnheim the title of genius, and is appointed to the station of craftsman: 'The technical means of expression of any art are limited; they become inexhaustible only under the hand of genius. . . . a Rembrandt. . . . the art of the perfect craftsman Sternberg exhausts itself in overnourishing the eye, while the spirit languishes.'

The intent of such reviews, whether positing the authorial originality of Jannings or of Sternberg, is not only to inscribe the presence of that subject holding communication with the spectator, but to define the particular terms of that subject: Jannings' tragic majesty, Sternberg's tortuous unreason. But such commentary is part of a process that does not stand still, and even in 1930 the importance of Jannings was giving way to that of Marlene Dietrich, who was beginning to be defined as creature-subject in relation to Sternberg as the creator-subject: we have Herman Weinberg's assurance, written in 1931, that *The Blue Angel*'s success in the United States 'was due principally to the presence of the exotic Marlene Dietrich (whom Paramount had already groomed and introduced as a star in *Morocco*) and in a lesser, though not unimportant degree to the direction of the American-assimilated Josef von Sternberg, who knew of the enormous reserve of sex-appeal dormant in the hitherto angelic Dietrich with which he pervaded his film.'[16]

This *knowledge* of Sternberg's, his special, unique insight, will become of over-riding importance in the commentary on his work. More clearly yet, in a review from Paris by Jean Lenauer (again from *La Revue du Cinéma*) one sees the terms of the relationship of author to audience: 'The film is great, rich, intelligent, but if Marlene Dietrich hadn't been there, we should never have been really taken with it. . . . *And it is necessary to be thankful to Sternberg for having shown us this extraordinary woman*' (emphasis added).[17]

Even Josef von Sternberg, however, was to be displaced by a commentary that had a particular ideological purpose and long-lasting effect on the way *The Blue Angel* would be regarded in ensuing years. Siegfried Kracauer erased Sternberg as the subject of the film's discourse, and seeming to deepen the resonances of subjectivity, placed in his stead 'the inner dispositions of the German people'.[18] Since the time that he had written his review of *The Blue Angel* for *Die Neue Rundschau* (translated in this volume), Kracauer had changed his opinion that the film was without significant relationship to the contemporary German social order. Certain factors came to prominence in the ghastly light of the Third Reich which in 1930 were without obvious significance, and the text of the film as rewritten in *From Caligari to Hitler* selects those particular signifiers which only acquired their 'true' signifieds in the years following the release of the film. Thus this passage about Rath's students: 'The boys are born Hitler youths, and the cockcrowing device is a modest contribution to a group of similar, if more ingenious, contrivances much used in Nazi concentration camps.'[19] This re-reading appears explicitly or implicitly in further work on *The Blue Angel* written after Kracauer.

Kracauer's late 'discovery' of the 'true meaning' of *The Blue Angel*, years after having described its hollowness, testifies to the ideological undercurrents of critical endeavour: at the end of the second devastating war with Germany within a generation, the Allies faced the task of reconstituting their relations with a state that could not be expunged from European history, cultural, economic, or political. The obscenity of the Third Reich could most acceptably be explained as a plunge into madness, and Kracauer's portrait of Germany seems significantly akin to that of the artist whose 'frenzy' André Sennwald had mentioned in 1934. What Siegfried Kracauer writes from America after World War II about a film made in Germany, should alert our reading of what Herbert Ihering has to say in the essay reproduced here about *An American Tragedy*, one of Sternberg's least regarded films, from his perspective in Germany just prior to Hitler's accession to power.

There is no lack of writing on the work of Josef von Sternberg. If the greater part of it is taken up by meditation on the 'relationship' between Sternberg and Dietrich, and if this meditation is a most decisive deflection away from the conditions of Sternberg's employment at Paramount, and from the manufacture and marketing of Marlene Dietrich as a commodity/image (Audibert, for example, tells us that for Sternberg, 'the look of the World became confused one day with the eyes of Marlene'), it suggests the importance of investigating that fascination itself as a component of the social order. The analysis of *Morocco* by the editorial collective of *Cahiers du Cinéma*, translated here, considers this factor in terms of an overinscribed fetishism, something which, if they attribute it to an effect of authorship on the one hand, to the working through of a masochistic fantasy by Sternberg himself in the guise of La Bessière, is recognised on the other hand as participating in the 'devaluing valuation' of women characteristic of the Western episteme, and which is permutated through erotic, social, racial, and topographic relationships in the film. It seems more than incidental that this essay's proposal of the vanishing object of desire, objectified in the last shots of the film, should find an analogy in Josef von Sternberg's estimation of 'glamor' in photography and on the screen, the principal aspect of which never changes: 'it promises something it cannot deliver.'

We are led back, by Barry Salt's essay, from fascinated apprehension before the promise made, to the material process of its making. Salt emphatically writes Sternberg's 'genius' into place, yet, in terms of the practice of the narrative cinema, his revelation of the astonishing rhythmic structure of *The Scarlet Empress* might usefully be considered along with the work of Audibert and Mackenzie in attempting to define both the complexity of the reaction the film elicits, and the concrete situation of its production. As a commodity the film was subject to practices peculiar to studio production, which could be inflected in certain ways by Sternberg from his position within those practices, turning out a film that does not escape its commodity identity, yet a film that offers itself as a body, flaunting itself before us, flirting with us, shimmering and flashing as Sophia Frederica dances down the stairway to her encounter with Count Alexei.

It is fitting, then, that Blaine Allan's essay on *The Saga of Anatahan*, the last in this collection, should deal with how he understands Sternberg's own voice, transformed into a voice of memory and experience, as binding the body of the visuals together, giving a significant order that would otherwise not be there, the order again (though in a different register) of that *knowledge* that belongs to the artist, and which Sternberg might be seen to claim for himself in speaking the commentary. Here is the film that perhaps more than any of his others seems to urge us to subject ourselves to the author's presence, the film in relation to which Sternberg identified himself as 'poet', the film marked by the 'detachment' that is 'Jovian', the privileged possession of the old man speaking from the Olympian summit of his experience (Luc Moullet had suggested this quality for Sternberg's *Jet Pilot*). Nevertheless, I should be inclined to argue that in the textual terms that Allan adopts for analysis of the function of that voice, the commentary is not a claiming but a surrender of sovereignty, that it does not mask the fragmentation of a narrative so much as articulate its members, that it does not enforce a singular reading but necessitates an active, reflective, and interminable engagement of its elements.

The point of this collection is to make available a number of texts in which a figure, 'Josef von Sternberg', has been inscribed, written into a sort of conceptual being, inscribed in human three-dimensionality and complexity from within the cultural apparatus and activity of an ideologically plural but hierarchical society. The specificity of this inscription, in its occurrence through history and at particular conjunctures, is crucial in locating our 'spontaneous' reactions to the films, and in delimiting what they have signified to us. 'Sternberg' is a complex imaginary image arising from a complex reality; both might be summed up in an anecdote told by the art director Boris Leven:

> The casino I built for *Shanghai Gesture* was enormous. Sternberg was riding the biggest boom in the world — he loved booms, you know, ever since Bill Ihnen, his art director on *Blonde Venus*, had ordered a boom without consulting Sternberg; Sternberg was astonished that anyone would try to supersede his authority, but he took a ride on it anyway, and loved it — and that's how legends, or self-images, are born. So on the *Shanghai Gesture* set, there was Sternberg on his boom, and he had a pocketful of silver dollars. Every time an actor did something that pleased Sternberg, he'd throw a silver dollar to him. The actor would go over, and slowly pick it up, and we would all feel terrible.[20]

As a reminiscence drawn from personal experience, this anecdote is imbued with testimonial value. Placed into circulation by *Film Comment*, it contributes to the production of a familiar, inexhaustibly fascinating image: the 'great Hollywood director', remembered as having himself become 'textual', a spectacle, a legend. At the same time, obliquely, the anecdote specifies the conditions from which the director's films, the director's legend, and eventually the fascination with that legend, arose: an advanced industrial technology, a hierarchical division of labour, and an embittering wage relationship. The difficulty of dealing with Josef von Sternberg, the man and the idea, as in dealing with any 'great Hollywood director', lies in according the proper value to each of these factors.

Notes

1. See Mark Nash, *Dreyer* (London; British Film Institute, 1977), p. 32.
2. Arnold Hauser, *The Social History of Art*, Vol. 4 (London; Routledge and Kegan Paul, 1962), p. 14.
3. Celia Simpson, 'The Cinema', *The Spectator*, No. 5, 329 (August 16, 1930), p. 214.
4. Evoe, 'At the Pictures', *Punch*, Vol. CLXXIX (August 20, 1930), p. 218.
5. Michael Sadleir, 'The Cinema in Germany', *The New Statesman*, Vol. XXXV, No. 902 (Saturday, August 9, 1930), p. 568. See also the ensuing correspondence.
6. Richard Dana Skinner, *'The Blue Angel'*, *The Commonweal*, Vol. XIII (December 31, 1930), p. 242.
7. Richard Demarcy, *Eléments d'une sociologie du spectacle* (Paris; Union Générale d'Editions, 1973), p. 351.
8. Paul Rotha, *The Film Till Now* (Feltham, Mddx.; Spring Books, 1967 [orig. pub. 1930]), p. 337.
9. See Curtis Harrington, 'The Dangerous Compromise', *Hollywood Quarterly*, Vol. III (1947–48), pp. 405–415.
10. André Sennwald, 'Josef von Sternberg, Stylist', *The New York Times*, September 23, 1934.
11. Ibid.
12. Rotha, op. cit., p. 193.
13. On 'hailing' see Louis Althusser, 'Ideology and Ideological State Apparatuses' in *Lenin and Philosophy and Other Essays* (London; New Left Books, 1971), pp. 162–165.
14. Ettore M. Margadonna, 'Errori di Sternberg', *Comoedia* (Milan), Vol. XV (January 1933), p. 39.
15. Ibid., p. 40.
16. Herman G. Weinberg, 'The Foreign Language Film in the United States: A Survey', *Close-Up*, Vol. X, No. 2 (1931), p. 167.
17. Quoted in René Jeanne and Charles Ford, *Histoire encyclopédique du cinéma*, Vol. IV: 'Le Cinéma parlant (1929–1945, sauf U.S.A.)' (Paris; S.E.D.E., 1958), p. 144.
18. Siegfried Kracauer, *From Caligari to Hitler: A Psychological History of the German Film* (Princeton; Princeton University Press, 1970 [orig. pub. 1947]), p. 11.
19. Ibid., p. 218.
20. Boris Leven in Mary Corliss and Carlos Clarens, 'Designed for Film: The Hollywood Art Director', *Film Comment*, Vol. 14, No. 3 (May–June 1978), p. 50.

GOSWIN DÖRFLER

Josef
von Sternberg's
Daughters of Vienna

(originally published in Filmkunst *(Vienna), No. 59, 1972, pp. 21–2)*

Josef von Sternberg, later the Hollywood director and discoverer of
Marlene Dietrich (which initially made him more famous than his own
film works, which were 'rediscovered' only shortly before his death) —
born Jonas Sternberg on the 29th May 1894 in Vienna II., Blumauer-
gasse 25, died 22nd December 1969 of heart failure in Hollywood's
Midway Hospital — spent his early childhood in Vienna, near the
Prater. Here he collected his first impressions, on which he also reports
at length in his autobiography *Fun in a Chinese Laundry* (published in
German in 1967 under the title *Ich Josef von Sternberg* by the Friedrich
Verlag, Velber bei Hannover). In 1901 his father called the family to join
him in America, having emigrated there himself four years earlier. But
the Sternbergs stayed in New York for only three years. Then they all
returned to Vienna: 'most probably because of my father's inability to
endure constant frustration. But not long after, like a squirrel that keeps
turning a cage, he once more left us to try his fortune, went again to the
same country, and again in vain', writes Josef von Sternberg in his
autobiography.

Again the capital of the Austrian regal and imperial monarchy
moulded the emotional world and the character of the young man, until
in 1908 the family again emigrated to America, this time for good. At first
Jonas Sternberg, who at 17 had his Christian name changed to Josef,
attended a high-school on Long Island; he became a handyman in a
fashion store, then in the store of a firm making lace goods until, after a
long period of unemployment, he became apprenticed to a man involved
in the chemical preparation and transportation of film material. He also
worked occasionally as a projectionist in a small cinema and finally
became the personal assistant to the production chief of the 'World Film
Corporation', where he was involved with the montage and editing of
film intertitles. When the USA entered the war he first assisted on some

10

army training films until in 1917 he himself served in the army, initially in the Signal Corps, then in the Medical Corps. After the war he returned for a short while to the World Film Corporation, then worked as an assistant director on other films, e.g. *The Mystery of the Yellow Room* (1919 — according to the Catalogue of Copyright Entries, The Library of Congress, 1951).

In 1921 — not 1922 as stated in the biographies — Sternberg returned to Europe (he first added the title 'von' in 1924, or rather it was introduced for the first time, initially without his knowledge and approval, in the credits of Roy William Neill's *By Divine Right*, on which Sternberg worked as assistant director and script writer). Sternberg does not mention this trip at all in his autobiography and in other Sternberg publications there is similarly nothing to be found, so it may be assumed that Sternberg did not work with the short-lived English 'Alliance Film Company', where he was amongst other things assistant director on *The Bohemian Girl* (1922), until *after* his Viennese trip.

At any rate, Sternberg stayed again in Vienna, for the first time after his emigration, from August 2nd till October 7th 1921, when he was officially registered in the 3rd precinct, Gärtnerstrasse 9, 3rd storey, door 15 as a film-director.[1] Here he met up again with a childhood acquaintance, the writer Karl Adolph. The latter, born 19th May 1869 — he died November 22nd 1931 in Vienna — emerged at the start of the twentieth century as the author of novels and sketches drawing on the proletarian life of the Viennese suburbs, which he was able to depict with a certain agreeable naturalism. His best known works are the novel *Haus Nr. 37* (1908), *Schackerl* (1912), *Töchter* (1914), and the tragi-comedy *Am I. Mai* (1919). Adolph, who was also a teacher, probably taught the young Sternberg.

Then in 1923 there appeared a book, *Daughters of Vienna*, freely translated from the Viennese of Karl Adolph by Jo Sternberg (printed by the art-printers Frisch & Co. (owner Ernst Wilhartitz) of the 3rd Vienna precinct in the autumn of 1922 under contract to a publisher, 'The International Editor London/New York/Vienna'). This is a translation of Adolph's novel *Töchter*, which appeared in 1914 in the Anzengruber Publishing House, Suschitzky Bros., Vienna and Leipzig, for which Karl Borschke designed the cover and Sternberg (address given as 57 Lloyd Avenue, Lynbrook, L. I., New York, U.S.A.) wrote the preface:

Vienna, November, 1922
I pilgrimed to the city of my youth, to find an old-fashioned man who knows its people better than any man alive today. I found the man, but alas! I no longer found the city. Vienna had been made a victim of a strange economic tangle engendered by the dreams of a few presumptuous statesmen. The beautiful city had become the cheap amusement-park of the world. In the face of an army of invaders, who,

regaled with light-hearted music, demanded that the city become one gigantic cabaret, the sons of Vienna were helpless, and many of its pretty daughters — well — starving is unpleasant.

To the casual observer, only the brilliancy (this morning I saw an old couple and a little boy, in rags all three, digging into a garbage-heap for food), only the wealth of color is visible, and unbelieving ears are turned to the frantic appeals for aid. And Vienna, or rather, (I dislike saying it) its carcass, decomposes, and the intense colors are the by-product of decay.

In this polychrome, the drab is hardly noticed. The old-fashioned man I had come to see, is one of the drab spots. Of the old school — nothing lurid, nothing mystic, nothing fantastic, nothing morbid is his. He loves the lowly, not only because he understands them, but also because he is one of them. His age is difficult to estimate, for he has the beard of a man and the eyes of a child. This mild and gentle man with the absent-minded appearance is Karl Adolph. His mind is still with the old Vienna. The new conditions, constantly changing, confuse and throw him out of contact with the city to which he belongs and which once belonged to him.

Knowing no more about me, than that I love Vienna, he gave me permission to change and paraphrase his brain-child at will. I asked him to tell where he had drawn his inspirations from to create his characters. He did not smile as he replied that his characters were not inspirations; they were real and he had come to know them through painting their homes. Painting their homes with a big brush. Literally painting their homes. He had been a wall-painter by profession.

And so let us listen for a few hours to this painter of walls and souls.

J.S.

When one reads Karl Adolph's book, and knows the work of Josef von Sternberg, one understands why it moved this imperious, fantastic, generous director. It depicts a world that was linked with Sternberg's youth and which influenced him all his life, in all his films. The same world to which another emigré was linked until his death far away, Erich von Stroheim, who likewise could never disown his origins in his films. Doesn't the following passage from Karl Adolph's *Töchter* sound like a sequence from a film-script, a direction for a film by Stroheim or Sternberg?

... Tini had her 'Graf.' A very old one, to be sure, for whom she really only provided amusement. But she had another five 'Grafs' besides, a handsome cavalry officer amongst them. And then sometimes her sculptor came to visit, who was by and large happy to be free of a lover he had grown tired of and only regretted the loss of the model. The writer was out of the question, since he had threadbare clothes and manners that were too unsophisticated and he could have hurt Tini who sometimes made the effort of speaking High German and playing the High Life lady.

Otherwise she ran a proper salon, had herself well entertained, showered the rays of her sun's favour over everyone who was able to satisfy Phyrne, and for the hundredth time sang '. . . I'm a tough cookie' to her old beau.

If any one thing ruled her lowly mind, it was the urge to impress all those who had once known her as 'the janitor's girl', as simply the Trümmler Tini, as the daughter of her plebeian-minded father (Tini imagined she had risen above the milieu she hailed from by her own efforts), as the sewing-girl — in short as a branch of an honourable, but in her eyes lower breed. (pp. 123–4.)

(translated by Nick Greenland)

Note

1. Josef von Sternberg's other periods of residence in Vienna before the annexation of Austria by Germany were from the 7th–17th December 1925, again Gärtnerstrasse 9 (registered as 'director'), from 8th–26th October 1937 in the Hotel Astoria (registered as 'businessman' and from the 3rd–10th January 1938, again in the Hotel Astoria (this time registered as 'director').

MORRIS GILBERT

Paris Cinema Chatter

REMARKABLE POPULARITY OF AMERICAN CROOK PICTURES —
OTHER SUCCESSFUL FILMS

(originally published in The New York Times, *April 20, 1930)*

Paris

Two films have been shown in Paris which seem to have a perpetual appeal, month in, month out. There is a 'cult' for them among the intellectuals and an undying enthusiasm for them among ordinary theatergoers. Both, as it happens, feature George Bancroft. One is *Nuits de Chicago,* known at home, I believe, as *Underworld.* The other is John Monk Saunder's *Docks of New York,* called here *Les Damnées de l'Océan.*

When it is written that the appeal of these two pictures is 'perpetual' it is hardly an exaggeration. *Nuits de Chicago* is on the permanent repertoire of Les Agriculteurs, where it is the most popular picture shown, according to M. Queyrel, director. It has two, sometimes more, showings every week. Besides, it drifts out into occasional weekly bookings in the neighborhood houses. The machine-gun siege of the Chicago gunman's tenement fort draws outright applause. The work of Bancroft never loses its power to magnetize this city, and Evelyn Brent is only a little less esteemed.

As for *Docks of New York,* it played as the chief attraction of Le Vieux Colombier for months and then suddenly dispersed itself all over Paris in the weekly run theaters, where it still makes one or more appearances each week.

The Vieux Colombier, on the street of that name on the left bank, has had a proud history, as every one knows, as an experimental theater. The curiously forlorn little house, lopsided because of a row of boxes extending all the way down one side, is the antithesis of the handsome new Paramount. Without the benefits of a daily stage 'show,' newsreel, animated cartoons, a big orchestra or sound apparatus; painted a revolting melancholy blue which might be green or gray; it is no place to go for whiling away a few moments unless you really expect to enjoy the picture. The theater is so depressing that the audience never speaks above a whisper in the intermissions, and the sexless voices of the vendors of sugared slices of orange, prunes and cherries (all very sticky on little strips of manila paper) resound like serenaders in purgatory.

But *The Docks of New York* filled this depressing spot night by night. Paris, which fifty years ago adored the Wild West, its peaux rouges and its bison, is equally avid today, one judges, for stories of the less creditable purlieus of the great cities across the Atlantic. The tale of the two stokers, the drifting girl, the roaring saloon beside the greasy East River, caught hold. Its popularity has not adversely affected the appreciation of it by the studious minds of the avant-garde. It fulfills their requirements, somewhat obscure to this reviewer, of rhythm, plasticity and unity. In simpler and more popular terms, it seems to be exceptionally good motion picture entertainment.

As for *Nuits de Chicago*, the piece was a furor. In the minds of those enterprisers of the serious film here in Paris — and it must be said that Paris offers much more opportunity for experiment, for artistic effort, for the cultivation of the cinema as an art, then New York does — the picture is a film classic.

As produced at Les Agriculteurs — where the house is sold out ahead of time whenever it is listed — there are, no doubt, various little alterations of scenes and climaxes as is the custom there. The orchestra of which they are so proud performs its own special obbligato to the story. The observer, as has been mentioned hitherto in these dispatches, sees the picture from the vantage point of an armchair as big as any President Doumergue might own. But the essence of the melo has not been changed in any way. It is the same thriller which America will remember. It simply happens to be, in all probability, the most popular film in Paris; and at the same time the film most applauded by the literati.

LOUIS CHAVANCE

The Case of Josef von Sternberg

(originally published in La Revue du Cinéma, *Vol. 2, No. 12 (1 July 1930), pp. 3–14)*

There is not the least relationship between Josef von Sternberg's life and the body of his work, or any one of his films. It would be amusing to draw contradictory lessons from these different realms, if I believed in the instructive value of vivid examples. Despite this, the director's handwriting is always recognizable, if only in the energetic confidence in the cinema that is so different from the willing destruction practiced by the best of our own friends. What I mean is that it is impossible to sketch the author's outline, as can be so easily done, and with so many charming arabesques, for a writer or a dramatic poet.

*   *   *

... In his beginnings at least, Sternberg seemed able to succeed only with desperate undertakings. *The Salvation Hunters, Underworld;* these films seemed destined for failure. The subjects he chooses are always related to some theme of distress. *The Exquisite Sinner* was the title of a film he did not complete for MGM. With Benjamin Glazer he wrote a scenario called *The Street of Sin.* Finally, *Underworld* and *The Docks of New York,* which he made afterwards, bear the mark of violence and rage. Such a tormented soul seems to approach as near as possible to what is called genius.

*   *   *

But it is no longer a question now of Josef von Sternberg. The director's personality and extraordinary power no longer enter the matter, any more than does his boundless ability to conjure up the beings he wants as he wants them, for the welcome given to *The Case of Lena Smith,* the last film of his that we have been able to see in Paris, shows that as far as certain subjects go, virtuosity has no effect on the public. The link

16

between *Underworld* and his later police films, such as *The Dragnet* and *Thunderbolt,* is finally broken. Sternberg disappears completely behind his work, and after each film one no longer recognizes him. Yet each film bears his mark. Not for him what for any other Creator would be called a 'power of renewal', the faculty of changing his identity and taking a pseudonym without anyone noticing the deception. He is always responsible for the inspiration, though he is no longer its originator. Such is the mystery, the case of Josef von Sternberg.

We ought to have noticed it a long time ago, here in France, despite the lack of continuity in the presentation of films, caused by the distance separating Paris from Los Angeles. We were able to see *The Docks of New York* a year ago; it's been eighteen months since *The Case of Lena Smith* was made; we ought to have realised in this time that the faults, the crevices, the rents spread through the works of a single director admit of no explanation. If we consider the succession of films in the order in which they were produced in Hollywood, we notice a singular unevenness of value: *The Salvation Hunters,* the revelation; the attempt with Mary Pickford; *The Exquisite Sinner*; the film for Edna Purviance — a series of disasters; *Underworld,* the thunder-clap; *The Last Command,* that garbage; *The Dragnet,* the humiliation of copying himself without success; *The Docks of New York,* or strength regained; *The Case of Lena Smith,* which upsets all forecasts; *Thunderbolt,* a talking film inert in its silent version. It is curious that he fails to rise to the challenge of the enumeration that criticism has performed in demonstrating its impotence before the Sternberg case. Absolutely none of the reasons that can be invoked to explain why some of his films are good and others bad has any logical probability.

One cannot propose favourable or unfavourable working conditions, for the way in which he surmounted the difficulties that beset the production of his first film proves that his energy soon disposes of material obstacles. The readjustment and the confusion of the talking film do not enter the picture: speech blossoms from the lips of all his characters, and the formidable nervous tension of their personalities unleashes words just as did the clean and precise gestures which at one time held the power of revelation. What resistance, or what facility does Sternberg meet with at each attempt? Intellectual complications do not obstruct his path. I consider as null and void that obligation that some seem to wish to impose upon him to treat *ad infinitum* the subject with which he once succeeded.*The scenario has no importance for him.* It has been justly remarked that the anecdotes drawn by analysis from his works would in other hands become the most revolting of penny-dreadful stories. It is all the more characteristic that the word 'calvary' can figure in one of his titles [the French title of *The Case of Lena Smith* was *Le Calvaire de Lena X* (ed.)] without being followed by that cascade of ridiculous and odious misfortunes which usually accompany it. I should not be astonished if *The Blue Angel*, the film that Sternberg has made in Germany, and the plot of which follows that alternation of stupid physical and mental satisfaction followed by the kind of degradation peculiar to Emil Jannings, belongs in spite of everything to his terrible and compressed style. Nor is there any moral question in the problem and his mystery. Sternberg is often reproached with an absence of position toward those forces that he places against each other, the police and gangsters, as if anarchism pushed to the uttermost and absolute amoralism needed qualification. His detectives no more represent society than his gangsters constitute a symbol of revolt. There are two sides to a situation. It is the stronger who carry the day, and it would be stupid to choose between the double constraint of order and disorder.

There is no cause which could explain the clear difference of quality between two films which follow immediately upon one another. There is no discernible continuity between these two successive phenomena, exaltation and disgrace. I cannot imagine that the same man should be shown capable of renewing his reserves of energy in order to release them in another way, after having once seemed to attain the limits of violence. These successive paroxysms go beyond what can be foreseen. In the first case Bancroft was met with in the form of a glorious brute. In its tendency to reify filmic figures, the public expected to find him always self-consistent. His next appearance was as a brutal sailor, at the breaking point from the strain of maintaining his own impassibility. Then James Hall sharpens a cynical smile in order to maintain forever the same superhuman severity. It is not the least merit of *The Case of Lena Smith* to lay down the same kind of strength for us, while completely changing the rules of the game. This intense capacity for bounding back, this agility is unsettling: the relationship is unclear.

And nevertheless the relationship exists. Everyone fell into the trap of believing that they had found in Bancroft the symbol of that unleashed force. Once the actor had departed, no one any longer understood. There are cold and hard actresses who put a kind of unity into the work, those straight and haughty women who look upon life only from under lowered lashes. No event breaks through their indifference. A grave accident occurs: they show no surprise. Their steely eyes glance towards crime without a movement of the head, then return slowly to their meditation. An incredible tension suddenly draws Sternberg's actress like a bow: love for the weakest, for the most debased, for one who hardly merits pity. This is the quality of mother love in *The Case of Lena Smith*. Time after time these women attain and lose their divinity. Evelyn Brent attracted an admiration that deserted her as soon as she stopped appearing in Sternberg's films. Betty Compson, Esther Ralston, Fay Wray become as beautiful as they are otherwise undistinguished. Marlene Dietrich, the star from whom they say *The Blue Angel* borrows the greater part of its interest, owes her charm to no one other than her director.

*   *   *

The Case of Lena Smith introduces us to the mystery, and gives us the key. Before it, one could believe in an alternation of successes and failures; the succession was informed by a rhythm that gave criticism some purchase. But Esther Ralston came into view, one of the most trivial of all the puppets used for comic or dramatic series. James Hall in no way fills the enormous place left vacant by Bancroft. The film seems wilfully disagreeable. I seem to see, in the perturbation it has caused me, a reason for finding more singular yet the question posed by its *mise en scène*. Here is the scene most characteristic of the work as a whole. A heavy silence reigns in the antechamber of the Bureau of Morals. The police themselves walk on tiptoe, and the petitioners have to rise and bow at the passage of important personages without making a sound. Esther Ralston rises. 'Shh! No noise!' She addresses the beadle; he puts a finger to his lips. All commotion is stopped by a barrier that only the emotional force of this woman is able to break down. Life, death, society, disorder, love, hatred: with Sternberg these never mean anything other than energy expended against an enormous weight of inertia. The strength he manifests is as directionless as it is cosmogonically possible to be.

This abstract force requires no application to any real or unreal event. Perhaps it exhausts itself all the more to the extent that its outpouring is applied to a more trifling sphere? In any case, it is utterly unimportant, and for my part I am completely indifferent, whether it is applied to something I find sympathetic or odious, so long as it exists, for its appearance no longer depends on anything but a certain psychological disposition. That is why it is also perfectly all right with me that Sternberg, a great anarchist, despises the act of destruction which seems indispensable to a certain degree of intellectual organisation. He feels no need to demolish, since black and white possess the same *intensity* in his eyes.

At bottom the personality of the individual is as null as the colour of the world around him. Everything that has seemed to me beautiful in Josef von Sternberg's existence is counter-balanced by uncongenial elements. He is an 'intellectual' and takes pleasure in publishing novels like the celebrated *Daughters of Vienna,* which made a sensation in the world of the American cinema. Nothing gives a better idea of his pretentions than the photographs published in Germany where he is shown nonchalantly stretched out on a divan, a book in his hand, enveloped in an ample velvet robe, under an immense painting in the most modern style. His subordinates find him proud and conceited. He has toyed with detective stories, and with maritime adventure, as he has rivalled Stroheim in the game of 'Vienna 1900.' All this is unimportant; I find his films admirable nonetheless. All I can concede to general opinion is that Sternberg no longer interests me in himself. The tiresome work of criticism ends in a vicious circle. The author of the films can be considered to be non-existent: he is a concept of unleashed force, as Bancroft, with less variety and suppleness, with more coarseness, is its visual symbol.

(translated by Peter Baxter)

SIEGFRIED KRACAUER

The Blue Angel

(originally published in Die Neue Rundschau *(Berlin), No. 41, Pt. 1 (June, 1930), pp. 861–3)*

It often happens in German public life that something appears on the scene that has been excellently made and has only one fault; namely that it is really nothing at all. It could not be more artistically put together but its trappings are mere ornament. Such empty show pieces are typical of our public life today. The concealed reason for this is that it holds nothing behind it.

A prime example of this lack of substance, which it would be worthwhile to analyse, is the film which has been so much praised in the press—*The Blue Angel*. It contains details that couldn't be better; it is built up and cut with undeniable skill. It must be admitted that it is an outstanding achievement; that the alternation between dialogue scenes and silent scenes confers on the film a special power which has never before been so penetratingly realised; that some scenes (e.g. that of the headmaster in the classroom or of the wedding breakfast) are extraordinarily conspicuous; that Jannings with the assurance of a well seasoned actor extracts every conceivable effect from anything that could possibly provide one; and that there is a pleasing harmony between Marlene Dietrich's vocal organs and beautiful legs. All this is admitted, but to what purpose the legs, the effects, the technique, the gigantic theatre?

For a private tragedy which in this version and today concerns no-one very much. The fact that Heinrich Mann's novel is misused is not a decisive factor here. More important is the fact that this pre-war book has been chosen at all as a basis. What interest led the film producers, who could equally well have chosen Mann's *Der Untertan*, to the dark psyche of Professor Unrat and his relations with the singer Lola? It was this: the subjects which are nowadays considered to be of interest betray the fact that they are not real subjects at all. The selection which is made of themes and structures may be conscious or unconscious, but nevertheless the aim is, as *The Blue Angel* testifies, to forget reality and to conceal it. The personal fate of Unrat is not an end in itself— much more than this it is just a means to an end—i.e. escape from reality, and in this respect is like the painting on the theatre curtain which gives the illusion of the play. Unfortunately the public never notices that the curtain is never raised.

But don't individual destinies and psychology exist now after the war as they did before? Certainly, and there would be nothing against their legitimate representation. Only, our film has nothing to do with the suitable unfolding of its theme. If it were to concern itself with that and nothing else the characters would then form part of a wider society; in fact the conditions which bring the grammar school teacher and the *'diseuse'* together would of themselves come into the foreground. For if we have learnt anything at all from the recent past it is this: that individual destinies where they seem undetermined, are in fact determined by the contemporary economic and social situation. This film, however, avoids, with an assiduity which must have been exhausting, any reference which could move us to include present social conditions. It suppresses the social environment which would force itself upon the naive spectator of Unrat's catastrophe, it tears the performers out of any social context in which they would have gained contemporary significance and places them in a vacuum. Neither Lola nor Unrat has enough air to breathe, which confirms the claim that it is less the reality of their existence that is to be demonstrated, than the existence of reality that is to be veiled.

So what seems to be questioned is not in question at all. But more than this; this futile shadow boxing is inflated to colossal significance. In this too *The Blue Angel* keeps to the rule that is valid here for most public events. One seeks through the use of monumental architecture to raise the illusion that the content which this architecture surrounds is indeed content. One places decorative walls in front of subjects which are only pretexts and claims that they are real subjects. With the same din with which savages drive away evil spirits people here want to stifle unpleasant realisations, i.e., realisations which make us conscious of that reality that we are fleeing from.

Whilst in truth Professor Unrat should disintegrate noiselessly, in the film he perishes with a great flourish. The spiritual events, which today more than ever seem to belong in a transparent casing, are dragged into the open and with optical and acoustic close-ups are turned into the main outward events: this has its justifications. If the outer conditions of our existence are to move out of our consciousness then the inner life must rush to fill out the external world, and develop into an ostentatious facade behind which the real exterior can disappear unnoticed. An inverted glove — the inside becomes the outside so that the outside is made invisible, and Jannings can crow as loudly as he likes. The appearance of lost inwardness which otherwise would serve no purpose is here just right as the substitute for outer reality.

Fortunately this reversal of the normal order of things avenges itself. Compared with the broad school scenes Unrat plunges downwards too suddenly and abruptly. This is what happens when one uses spiritual events as decoration: their continuity is not always transferable. Also the intent desire of the artificial harbour street to be expressive long after

Expressionism is deceiving. It subjects itself freely to psychic invasion: it is reduced to the level of decor. And finally the screeching and clattering; the sadism and the battle cries at the end: what a hopeless comparison between hullabaloo and meaning is set up here. But the hullabaloo is required to conceal the lack of meaning.

The success of *The Blue Angel* in covering up our situation by thundering over it and thus escaping it, is in itself a characteristic of this situation. For those strata which determine the face of German public life there is nothing left but to cloud reality. They have no vital perceptions with which to counter attacks from the opposition. They find themselves, as I have pointed out in my book, *The Employees*, [*Die Angestellten* (1930)], ideologically on the defensive. Therefore in their own interests they cannot permit public debate about the fundamentals of the existing situation. How the dangers of such debate are exorcized is shown by the exemplary case of *The Blue Angel*. It shows, too, that in the long run all attempts to escape are in vain as they lead to a gaping void.

(translated by Jill Dimmock)

Published by permission of Suhrkamp Verlag, Frankfurt.

The Blue Angel and An American Tragedy

(originally published in Berliner Börsen-Courier, *these reviews were reprinted in* Von Reinhardt Bis Brecht, *Vol. III, 1930–1932 (Berlin; Aufbau-Verlag, 1961))*

The Blue Angel   2 April 1930

After the success of this new Ufa talking picture the situation is much clearer. Josef von Sternberg has brought with him his American experiences in talking pictures and developed them further in the technically magnificent Neubabelsberg studios. The direction of the Talking picture is now apparent. Its laws are being defined.

The continued technical development of the talking picture has never been doubted here. That the invention would make progress was already clear many years ago when the first primitive experiments were shown. However, the cultural evaluation of every technical achievement is dependent on the intellectual content it serves: what it promotes, what it furthers, what it allows to die. It's no coincidence, therefore, that the first German talking picture to bring the formal principle clearly into focus is simultaneously the first talking picture whose subject-matter has input from intellectual and artistic spheres (if not from the sphere of life). The talking-picture is a principle in subject-matter as well as a technical and formal principle.

The Blue Angel is based on Heinrich Mann's novel *Professor Unrat.* Carl Zuckmayer and Karl Vollmoeller wrote the manuscript (Robert Liebmann the film-script). For the first time it's possible to speak of authors and talking pictures. The introduction of intelligence [*'Geist'*] into film. Erich Pommer should not be belittled for this achievement. With the theme from Heinrich Mann responsibility to literature grew. It was no longer possible to launch out into the boundless, the superficial. At most, epic theme and film drama were not always brought into harmony.

An instructive example. Where the film develops the theme organically — the hide-bound high-school pedant by pursuing his pupils finds himself in the harbour-dive, 'The Blue Angel', and is totally disoriented by the music-hall girl Lola Lola — the cinematographic problem too is completely solved. Systematically, and in accordance with a principle,

24

Josef von Sternberg makes use of alternation of sound and silence, loud and soft. He knows that it isn't necessary to talk all the time. He knows that sound is only effective when it's followed by silence. Sound for him is not imitation of reality, but a dramaturgical, formal, stylistic principle. Professor Immanuel Rath enters the 'Blue Angel' for the first time. The door opens, a whirl of sound hits him. Another door opens, more confusion of voices. A door swings to, it grows quieter. The second door swings to, it's silent. Or: footsteps. One time they can be heard. Another time not. It's always compositional laws that are at work, not haphazard reality.

But the film-script still feels obliged to present 'Professor Unrat's' downfall in accordance with cinematographic convention, thus bypassing the theme. Professor Unrat becomes a clown and, just as he wants to show off, his woman deceives him. Again 'laughter, buffoon'. But this is avenged. For now, of necessity convention intervenes. Now the epic ensemble film turns into the dramatic star-vehicle. Solo number for Emil Jannings. Grandiose solo number. Jannings has to cry cock-a-doodle-doo. And this cry becomes a screeching, raving, piercing cry of madness. Again and again. Again and again. This cry is staggering because it erupts from the silence. But: the talking picture is a critique of the star. Jannings is exceptional at the point where the embittered pedant breaks free of inflexibility, where rigidity for the first time softens into smiles. Later the film becomes too strongly focused on Jannings. Jannings acts too obtrusively. He uses the necessary alternation of sound and silence for his own intricately prepared effects. That hampers the pace and disturbs the total composition.

This film is thus stronger in the composition of the individual scenes than in the composition of the whole. Retarding elements can seemingly not be made good by later cuts. Certain aspects seem to have been conceived by Jannings too much as a stage role. He declaims. That involuntarily evoked memories of his theatrical roles. There it is: precisely the fear people had about the talking picture. It endangers itself by competing with the theatre. The talking picture will never be able to eradicate live theatre, not even in the provinces.

The revelation: Marlene Dietrich. She sings and acts almost without involvement, unemotionally. But this sensual lack of emotion is stimulating. She's vulgar without acting. It's pure cinema, nothing is theatrical. For the first time in talking pictures a female voice comes across with timbre, tonal colour, expression. Extraordinary. Otherwise it's a disapointment. Kurt Gerron, undefined, in too much of a hurry. Rosa Valetti too still lacks self-confidence. Surprisingly, Eduard von Winterstein has a good talking picture voice.

So: even less than the silent film can the talking picture afford to be a star vehicle. But the silent film retains its particular tasks alongside the talking picture. These were indicated by the director Carl Junghans in the film *Such is Life* [*So is das Leben*, 1929]. *People on Sunday* [*Menschen am Sonntag*; dir. Robert Siodmak and Edgar Ulmer, 1929] proved them. The talking picture enriches film. It's not a replacement for the silent film.

(translated by Nick Greenland)

* * *

An American Tragedy   8 October 1931
Yesterday Paramount arranged a special screening of the film *An American Tragedy*, which, as is known, Josef von Sternberg has adapted from Theodore Dreiser's novel. I do not know Dreiser's work in enough detail to be able to take a stand in the quarrel over to what degree Sternberg has done justice to Dreiser. But I do know that the film, in and of itself, is a masterpiece — and not only in and of itself. For, just as it is certain that Sternberg needed material other than the ordinary Hollywood faces, and also took advantage of Dreiser's themes, so is it certain that he has made a film that really presents an American destiny; represented in the life of a young man who uses women to climb up in society, who falls and is detroyed because of a murder.

A young man's hollowness and frivolousness. But the way this is presented in the film! One forgets the Sternberg of *The Last Command* (mendacious, novelistic kitsch inhibits him as an artist). Here: veracity gives him wings! In the hotel, in the simple apartment, in society, on the water, in the street — what richness of images, which never become their own goal; what richness of exquisite faces, which represent an American world. The economy and lightness of the acting! The precision and agility! This artistic freedom, this artistic feeling — and yet the criticism is razor-sharp, the rejection of a world is accomplished through representation alone. Josef von Sternberg: almost the only example of the fact that it is possible to make art enjoyable and yet critically reject the world represented in it.

This film must be shown publicly in Germany ... As is known, there is also a theatrical version by Piscator of *An American Tragedy*, which should be shown at the Lessing Theatre. The film would be the best kind of complement to the evening at the theatre, and the latter could serve as a gloss to the film.

(translated by Maaret Koskinen)

* * *

23 April 1932
It has taken a long time for Josef von Sternberg's Dreiser film to be shown publicly in Berlin. On the occasion of a private screening I referred to this work last October. In the meantime, new films have kept coming to Germany, which, true enough, show often-brilliant execution of technique and acting, but also the thematic untruthfulness of the

American cinema. Films that oscillate between bigotry and the heroising of crime, that idealise a world of false virtues and false 'supermen', while they do not achieve the style of presentation that points out the hypocrisy, or criticises it through the form of the rendering. Even a thriller such as *City Streets* [dir. Rouben Mamoulian; Paramount, 1931] (in itself splendidly realised) belongs to this dangerous species of film.

One never reaches a critical distance in the American film. In its place treads a moralising philosophy of adaptability, which is the more ineffectual in that every thief and swindler knows perfectly well how to match it with his actions. When one surrenders to admiration for the exercise of power and the courage of bootleggers, to the brilliant cunning of hired killers, then it is difficult to extinguish this impression with morally constructive speeches. What one sees — the whacking great car chases, the elaborate break-ins, the escape over the rooftops and across rivers — is stronger than the sourish preaching that one hears, or even the walk into prison, that one sees but does not believe. Gangster films with tacked-on morals always proselytise for the gangster, if the presentation of the gangster does not in itself prevent idealisation. But this is only possible when the social structure in which the crime takes place is shown clearly; when the gangster is shown not as a vagabond adventurer, but as a social outcast. In repressing this social criticism (out of fear, crushing it), the American film truly does itself an injury, even business-wise, for the fear of the truth removes its internationality from it. In Europe, the resistance to it is stiffening.

The more worthwhile is a Paramount film like Sternberg's *An American Tragedy*. It may be that here, too, the social criticism could have been more sharply worked out. Even so, this film is one of the few examples of what I said earlier: that a world that is enjoyably presented with artistic means can still be critically distanced and rejected. This is why this film remains wonderful. Wonderful in its unprejudiced, almost fragmented detachment, in its cool beauty, in its fabulous acting. Phillips Holmes is superb as the weak type, as the irresolute 'climber' who stands between classes and wants to rise in society. He lacks only the capacity to be more supple with his role in terms of acting techniques, and to vary it physically. Sylvia Sidney is, as in *City Streets,* unequalled in conveying quiet urgency. A real artist, obeyed by every nerve of her animated face; a legitimization of the American cinema!

This film shows (disregarding its final images) where the American cinema must go in order to gain acceptance in the world. It does not have to resign itself to the means of suspense or the techniques of violence. It must change its focus and not tack on its criticism in the shape of morals, but instead, work from within the terms of representation itself.

Tonight, Das Marmorhaus has reached a new importance as a premier theatre.

(translated by Maaret Koskinen)

B. G. BRAVER-MANN

Josef
von Sternberg

(originally published in Experimental Cinema, *Vol. 1, No. 5 (1934), pp. 17–21)*

I

'Oh Hollywood, my beloved Hollywood!'

This rapturous exclamation falls from the lips of a small dumpy man with flowing sandy hair as he stands before his home on one of the hills that look down upon Hollywood's film factories. The little man lends a touch of the exotic and dramatic to his fervent declaration, for he wears a richly ornamented black velvet coat and his arms are outstretched as if offering a benediction.

The man is Josef von Sternberg. The time: 1927, the year in which his *Underworld,* a gangster film, was breaking box office records.

Underworld appeared at a psychological moment when people, wearied to a point of ennui by Hollywood's innocuous celluloid, were turning their attentions to news about the exploits and acquisitive technique of racketeers in the lower brackets. Appealing to the violent bourgeois desire of getting something for nothing, but getting it at the point of a gun if necessary, *Underworld* became a hit. This motion picture glorified the gangster; Sternberg's false fantasy, based on a Nick Carter conception of social reality, gave the picture an effective if cheap brand of melodrama. His own irrational appraisal of the immediate acceptance of *Underworld* in a society in which art stagnates simultaneously with the economic and political disintegration of capitalism, led Sternberg to exaggerate grossly the importance of this picture and himself to film art. He began to regard himself as *the* director in Hollywood. He implies that he is the messiah of film art in Hollywood. Hence, Hollywood should follow his methodology. His directorial colleagues he views with arrogance and disdain, although in both structure and content his work is just as slipshod and false as theirs. He continues to set himself up as an oracle of film opinion and from time to time issues statements on the cinema which should interest psychiatrists. He has thumbed his nose in public at Theodore Dreiser and Bernard Shaw whose social commentaries, although

28

appreciated by many high school boys, would probably leave Sternberg distraught if he really tried to comprehend them. The backwardness of the Hollywood cinema and of Sternberg, as its self-appointed spokesman and as a director, is exemplified in one of his statements which illustrates a penchant for putting fictitious above intrinsic values in film practice:

Hollywood has absolutely nothing to learn in motion pictures from any European country, neither from Russia or Germany.

This statement, like the outburst from his own hilltop, 'Oh Hollywood, my beloved Hollywood', is pregnant with connotations at once amusing and pathetic, for to observant film practitioner and layman alike it is plain that both of these messianic-Sternbergian remarks could be uttered only by a director who lacks sensitivity, who has a low standard of esthetic evaluation and an unbalanced philosophy of life and cinema. [. . .]

From the time Sternberg made *Salvation Hunters* down to the present day, he has persistently posed as an artist, an affectation which afflicts a considerable number of Hollywood's 'leading' directors, among them such over-rated men as King Vidor, Frank Borzage, C. B. De Mille, Clarence Brown and others whose chief claim to film leadership is rooted in their talent for *Kitsch*. Their work and Sternberg's are marked by a very narrow range in the use of the film's structural forms — a range so limited and inexpressive that aside from variations of subject matter their productions may pass for the output of one and the same director. None of Hollywood's directorial pretenders, however, has been as successful as Sternberg in transforming an affectation into a generally accepted myth about an artistry which exists in none of his films.

II

A film director is an artist in a complete sense when he employs his tools to present a dialectic treatment of nature and man, instead of picturing nature and man in a falsely romantic relation to each other; he seeks to develop new aspects of cinematic design in time and linear patterns and image relationships, with which to intensify artistically the deeply realistic content of his thematic material; he seeks new forms and methods not for their formal values alone but for their integration with an understanding of social phenomena, so that he may develop effective, and if possible, heroic image ideas. Judged by this standard, what is the position of Josef von Sternberg as a director?

In Sternberg we have a director who concentrates on surface effects, who emphasizes the externals of film mechanics in a most inarticulate manner and represents his own delirious fancies as real life.

This highly publicized director has been connected with motion

29

pictures for almost twenty years. He served as camera man [*sic*], film cutter and scenarist before becoming a director. But what of his actual performance?

His productions show that experience as a camera man is no guarantee that this practitioner can use or direct the camera filmically; that having been a film cutter is no proof that a man has film-organizational mastery, and that having written scenarios is no indication of the capacity for conceiving themes based on a sensitivity to social experience on one hand and dynamic cinematic form on the other.

What if Sternberg has been a camera man? The tricks and tonality of his photography are repetitive and monotonous, devoid of both inner meaning and pattern indicative of feeling for screen design, and, in short, without style. Curiously enough, he and pseudo-aesthetic critics label his camera direction as the work of a 'Stylist'.

What if Sternberg has graduated from the cutting room? His cutting — he has boasted to me that he cuts all his films — is among the worst examples of the simple linkage method, the most backward and unfilmic way of mounting film images and one that requires the least intellectual effort. The slipshod connection of the shots in his films shows a montage which fails to conceal this director's incredible ignorance of cutting. His films are completely lacking in that irresistible tempo and rhythm which mark the montage of great films.

What if he has been a scenarist? His scenarios — he writes them for his films[1] — call for a trivial methodology. They are given over to the propagation of gloomy vagaries without psychological and social insight. The inference is that a scenarist who deliberately writes such scripts must lack intellectual honesty. But a scenarist who produces them without knowing how dishonest his material is, to speak charitably, is simply ignorant.

Sternberg cannot be accused of lacking a sense of integrity and honesty within the framework of his own distorted outlook, since he has fought, on occasion, in behalf of what he considers to be right. In one instance he walked out of a studio rather than compromise with what he thought were his convictions. Sternberg, however, is honest in that he believes in his own ignorance. Yet his natural inclination to wallow in it is hardly a valid enough reason for expecting the spectator to accept the ephemeral world and empty fantasies of his work, no matter how much he may believe in them himself. [. . .]

A director so sadly limited, technically and intellectually, as Sternberg appears to be must needs lean upon two props in order to get by with his distortions of reality which gibe so nicely with the degenerate idealogy [*sic*] of the bourgeois cinema. These two props are (1) Pictorialism for its own sake and (2) player 'personality'. In this respect, Sternberg is no different than his directorial contemporaries in Hollywood whom he regards patronizingly. Although his pictorial talent is more developed than that of the majority of Hollywood directors, it is thin when compared with the grandeur of the pictorialisms in Murnau's *Faust* and *Dracula*. Moreover, Murnau, in addition to possessing the ability for imparting remarkable rhythm and continuity to his films, usually employed his richly pictorial mind for the exposition of plausible mood or situation. Beside the arbitrarily selected patterns of the images by Dovzhenko, Dreyer or Eisenstein, Sternberg's little pictorial talent is analogous to an insipid magazine illustration in contrast with a mural by Rivera or Orozco. The scenes in the productions by Hollywood's messiah of film art are very much like the first attempts of arty film amateurs who play with light, shadow and tone around, under and above objects with complete indifference to any inner meaning of the images. There may have been a time when Sternberg may have fitted into the field of illustrative photography — a field in which he properly belongs rather than in motion pictures — but advances among photographers in their approach to the object have become so forthright that it is doubtful whether he could hold his own among them today.

Sternberg's pictorialisms rarely conceal his poverty in film-structural invention and forced, pretentious direction of players, light and camera. His concern with the pictorial for its own sake is one of the reasons why no Sternberg film ever presents an image with a relationship to another image for the purpose of developing an independent image idea[2] in the mind of the spectator, thereby enabling the spectator to discover for himself the significance of a situation or idea. He is not equipped artistically, technically or mentally to build a film having the montage structure of such a picture as young Raisman's *In Old Siberia,* a Soviet film of minor importance. [. . .]

Sternberg's directorial incoherence and lack of proportion in dramatic values, due to his ignorance of the relation of man to his environment, are evident in his mechanical, schematic handling of players. They always strut. Whether the picture be *Underworld, The Docks of New York, The Blue Angel, Morocco, Dishonored,* or *An American Tragedy,* the women are always pushing each other or posturing about with hands on their hips. Olga Baclanova, a better interpreter of character and pace than Sternberg, and Emil Jannings, are the only players who have successfully rebelled at Sternberg's inability to probe human types in relation to environment and behavior. The players in his films strut — his pictures may be called *strutting* pictures — because he cannot build up image concepts and patterns with fragments of objects for the intensification of an idea or an emotion. His players must needs strut because the falseness of the content in his scenarios makes it impossible for him to cut a film so that it may present the greatest number of image ideas in the running time of the picture — even if he were able to cut a film in this manner. He *moves* instead of *cuts,* which is typical of all directors who build their films either in the non-cinematic pictorial and semi-theatre traditions of the motion picture. Sternberg's players strut because he cannot use the camera filmically for the selection of significantly graded and related images in time and space.

III

[. . .] *Salvation Hunters* was the first film directed by Sternberg. It was an independent venture by Sternberg, featured by such vicissitudes as lack of funds, materials, and even food, for the director frequently did not have money for his lunches, all of which should have made Sternberg curious about the contradictions in a society in which creative effort is virtually hamstrung.

Although Sternberg assured the writer that *Salvation Hunters* was an effort of which he was ashamed, it appears that he has reversed his position and declared to others that he considers this his best picture. *Salvation Hunters* was made after Stroheim's *Greed* began shocking the acquisitive instincts of the bourgeoisie and the petty-bourgeoisie. The visual grimness of the objects, locales and characters in *Greed* was interwoven with the ideological content of the film. In *Salvation Hunters*, however, Sternberg sought to imitate the optical realism of *Greed* for a theme that was the antithesis of Stroheim's picture. The caprice of the arty poseur — the fitful treatment of objects, players, camera and cutting — were unfolded in every shot. The sombre tonality of the mud, the dirt, the wharves and the water with its patterns of shimmering light were interesting only as photographic illustrations. As for having any montage value they were negligible. These shots showed that it is more important for a film to contain a powerful montage of image ideas even if it dispense with artistic photography than to consist of 'arty' images recorded for their own sake with indifference to their filmic organization.

Thus, in his first directorial effort Sternberg revealed he was unaware that the conclusion of his theme was artificial and its montage the antithesis of dynamic constructive cutting. The tedious pace and long scenes of the picture, tiresome because they contained none of the tension and situation that justify long scenes, set forth Sternberg's deficiencies in film structures although up to the time he made this film he had worked at various jobs around film studios for twelve or thirteen years. It is also pertinent to add that the slow pace of his films suggests a feverish straining after a dignity entirely absent in the dope-laden content of his themes. But as *Salvation Hunters* cost $5,000 one suspects that it was produced to show film magnates how cheaply a film might be manufactured. Sternberg succeeded in his objective since the film culminated in a directorial job with Metro-Goldwyn-Mayer.

However, in essentials Sternberg has been dead on his feet ever since he made *Salvation Hunters*. Bad montage and an amazing ignorance of the moving forces behind human behavior and social reality cluttered up his subsequent films — *The Dragnet, The Last Command, The Docks of New York, The Case of Lena Smith*, all silent films, and such talkies as *The Blue Angel, Dishonored, Morocco, An American Tragedy, Shanghai Express* and *Blonde Venus*. Sternberg has nothing to learn in motion pictures but in *Shanghai Express* he flattered Trauberg and Dovzhenko, the former by imitating *China Express* both in genre and action while from Dovzhenko's *Arsenal* he adapted clichés from the freight train sequence. But the imitation of vital formal methods is inherent in a failure to realize that they also represent an elucidation of man and his relationship to his immediate world.

Of course, the Hollywood cinema is so regimented that a dialectic analysis of social reality, artistically elucidated, is well nigh impossible. Nevertheless there are opportunities for a director even in Hollywood, if he have the will, ability and perception to single out incidents and situations in his thematic material which he may convert into images of social experience and give them vigorous filmic form. That this can be done is shown by Rowland Brown's *Quick Millions*, one of the few masterfully mounted pictures that have come from Hollywood.

But Sternberg has neither consciousness of reality nor consciousness of film form, both of which impel a director to create a film reality.

It is well to note here that an ultra-reactionary organization like The Daughters of the American Revolution was keen enough to put its finger upon the social challenge to bourgeois religion, morals, economics and law in Dreiser's *An American Tragedy*. [. . .] But all that Sternberg saw in Dreiser's novel was an illicit sex affair which ended in two killings, one of the girl by the young man and the other of the young man by the law. That bourgeois society molded and then by law murdered a young man reared in its image, escaped Sternberg. For that matter, there is not a single so-called 'big' director in Hollywood who is intellectually, technically and artistically qualified to do justice to the theme in Dreiser's novel. The only director — Eisenstein — who was thus qualified was rejected by the American film industry. So great was Sternberg's exultation at the humiliation of a fine motion picture artist that after being assigned the picturization of *An American Tragedy* he arrogantly proclaimed that 'Hollywood (meaning Sternberg?) has absolutely nothing to learn in motion pictures'. Such defiance had in it too much the note of fear — the consternation of a novice lest a film made on American soil by Eisenstein would have sharply exposed the backward status of Hollywood cinema. Furthermore, Sternberg sought to conceal his own failure to understand Dreiser's social interpretation by confusing the controversy between Paramount and Dreiser with statements to the effect that all the content of so long a novel as *An*

American Tragedy could not be filmed. And Ray Long, at the time already released from Hearst's editorial stables, erstwhile book publisher and now a story buyer for a film studio, also hauled out an opinion from the depths of his dubious profundity which amounted to a defense of Sternberg's attempt to camouflage his own unfamiliarity with social reality.

[. . .] Eisenstein's exit from Hollywood holds one clear implication — namely that Sternberg and the other 'leading', 'eminent' film maestros of Hollywood could not risk the inevitable reaction which would have followed the showing of an American-Eisenstein film in American film houses. The presence of Eisenstein in Hollywood meant that the tinsel foundations of Sternberg's and of many other directorial reputations in Hollywood were threatened!!! And *that could not be!* How the colony must have rejoiced at Eisenstein's exit. Who knows but that in their degradation they may have echoed the Sternbergian refrains of 'Hollywood has nothing to learn' and 'Oh Hollywood, my beloved Hollywood!' — the Hollywood which is being destroyed by its own incompetence and the general crisis now shaking the foundations of capitalist society.

Notes

1. This seeming privilege is reserved for 'leading' Hollywood directors because they can be depended upon to embody all those ingredients in a scenario which gives a picture maximum appeal at the box office and to the region below the belt but none above the neckline.
2. To be fair to Sternberg, we may recall the one and only instance of this montage in the many films he has made. This occured in *The Case of Lena Smith,* viz., the scene of the man taking a revolver out of the dresser drawer, which cuts to a scene of the smoke floating past the dresser drawer but with the man out of the picture. The implication, of course, is obvious — namely that the man killed himself during the interval between the two scenes. This set all Hollywood astir, and Welford Beaton in his *Film Spectator* pronounced this mounting as an example of 'brains'. However, it is more than likely that his use of contrast between two shots, elementary as it was, was due to one of the Elder Will Hays' dicta that suicides must not be portrayed too explicitly upon the screen.

RUDOLF ARNHEIM

Josef
von Sternberg

(originally published in Scenario *(Rome), No. 2 (1934), pp. 61–8)*

A great deal has already been written about Hollywood. The attentive reader of film periodicals knows the depth of the swimming pool at Buster Keaton's mansion, and the value of the authentic 18th century canopied bed that a famous director has had specially imported from France to rest upon at night away from all the canopied beds he has to deal with during the day. Some more assiduous readers will have also read a good many details on the manufacture of art as it is practiced in Hollywood. Nevertheless, we could also ask ourselves if Hollywood does not represent the purest and at the same time the most grotesque incarnation of a practice and of a conception of art that has dominated our whole culture right from the beginning of modern times, and that, despite having given an opportunity to some striking talents to create outstanding masterpieces, in the last analysis is fated to end badly. Will Hollywood mark this culminating point?

From the painter who for the first time, while speaking of depicting a Madonna, was photographing a charming, profane, bourgeois girl; to the French painters of the last century who boasted of being indifferent to whether they painted a Madonna or a horse; right up to the 'studios' of Hollywood where interest in the object — that is, relationship to life — has completely disappeared; to the sophisticated 'visual' men to whom even the profane and the earthly have become matters of indifference, and for whom pain, joy, and struggle are reduced to nothing more than a pretext for the fabrication of picturesque black and white images, for the exhibition of well-made bodies; is that not, in substance, the route already covered? Is there nothing wrong with such a conception of art, if after coming so far it is going to finish in the most facile and superficial epicurism?

An art that has lost its content: the expression of a humanity that has warded off all the great problems of life; that has made of religion, of politics, of the thirst for knowledge, so many questions for experts; that, having done so, has resolved the mysteries of the universe only with legal formulae; that in the place of joy and of exaltation has nothing better

35

than excitement, in the place of sorrow has nothing better than anger; in sum, fragments of men. In comparing an artist like Michaelangelo or Rembrandt with one who, like Cezanne, is of the same authority as far as skill is concerned, one sees clearly how in the first case the language of colours expresses a lofty spiritual world, while in the second case it adorns with all its splendour benign landscapes and women's bodies scattered here and there (petit-bourgeois taste, and a gifted eye).

Such a process of course culminates in America, where there is no tradition to serve as a brake: there where everything is easy, rational, progressive, everything can be brought cheaply; where the closest relationships are marked by cards already printed with congratulations, condolences, and New Year's greetings. There that art without roots could put forth its most gaily-coloured flowers: in the most fertile, sunniest region of that country, where the fruit is enormous, tender, and gorgeous, and tasteless and bland nevertheless: there, among the rich. If the old aesthetics established the enjoyment of art as 'disinterested pleasure', if it had intended to keep art far from good and evil, from truth and falsehood, it was as a matter of culture and of aristocracy. Hollywood, the plebeian, heedless and uncultured, would take the consequences without qualms, and reduce pleasure to 'sex-appeal', disinterest to frigidity. California unmasks Kant.

Nothing in this world attracts the heart of the men of Hollywood; everything attracts their eye. They live on paradisiacal golf courses; they see poverty on the emaciated faces of film extras; they know the picturesque design of peeling walls, the lustre of a street bathed in night. They have the most prestigious photographers, the best sound technicians at their service; in the studios these men create for them the smoke of cannons, the thickened air of a dockside tavern, the cry of a lone beast in the desert. But none of this is necessary, nor would any of it be necessary, except as the head of production makes it so. These men play at 'creation' as they play at golf; they almost try to outdo God Almighty. And they enchant us, until at last a shiver goes through us: we've understood the trick.

Even inharmonious men are capable of creating art; perhaps only inharmonious men, inasmuch as harmonious men have too few reasons to make art. Artists can even be unnatural men, dissipated, ruined. But, however, they cannot lack intense feelings, be atrophied and dulled. Hollywood, though, is unaware of what it lacks. In Hollywood no one is sufficiently honest, intelligent, or cultured to realise that the hoaxes of the 'studios' are not world history.

There, the approach of two mouths is a kiss; eyes turned to the heavens express passion; the jump from the scaffold is a tragedy. This is painful for a sensitive European: the substitution of the most brazenly superficial gesture for real feelings. Hell, Purgatory, and Paradise, manufactured like industrial products, on the basis of precise calculations; coldly.

36

And then there arrives in Hollywood one of these sensitive Europeans, and after years of wearying effort, he succeeds in having himself entrusted with the manufacture of important, costly films. What will come of this?

* * *

Unfortunately the history of the cinema is written with purple ink: the heads of the printing office are busied in propagating stories *ad majorem gloriam* of the 'star.' However, it is certain that Josef von Sternberg, born in 1894 in Vienna, was for years a 'cutter', a craft experience that only a few directors have today, and thanks to which a kind of world champion of editing. With 5000 borrowed dollars, he made a film in 1924, *The Salvation Hunters,* which for reasons of economy was filmed entirely on location, and in which, as he once told me, one of the principal parts was a huge crane.

This crane, with its gaping jaws like a prehistoric beast, already indicates a salient characteristic of all Sternberg's films: the important part played by objects, inanimate things, which, by showing the effects of human actions or symbolically reflecting the human, become the most powerful means of cinematic expression. We shall yet have occasion to discuss this art of freeing the human face of its mimicking function by occupying the hands of the actor with a series of characteristic objects which permit him to externalise his emotions.

Charlie Chaplin, Douglas Fairbanks, and Mary Pickford saw *The Salvation Hunters* in a private showing, and were so impressed by it that their company, United Artists, bought the film. The first step was taken. Now Sternberg had the chance to make two big films, *Underworld* and *The Docks of New York,* with George Bancroft, who had attracted little notice up till then, and with this film gained world fame for himself.

These films treat the Herculean exploits of a good giant in the Augean stables of dockside taverns and dens of iniquity. It might be said that no human type and no atmosphere could be more foreign to Josef von Sternberg. Indeed, what wondrous power of intuition was developed in such films by this ailing and sensitive man, the typical example of a western European intellectual! Instead of the naturalness of a gigantic sailor, he is gifted with all the critical control of an intellectual; he is cynical instead of innocent; introspective instead of awkwardly expansive; a man gentle and sensitive by nature, who gives the effect of having led himself into the long struggle against the wiliness and the stubborness of the film merchants, without in any way losing his original nature, and of now having become as ductile and as strong as a bar of steel. And this man had George Bancroft play the part of a sinewy Parsifal in so natural, simple, and true a way as almost to suggest that he, the director, were made of the same stuff.

One must agree with Freudian theories of art in that all artists create in their works human types opposite to their own natures. Nietzsche was not a blonde beast. Wagner possessed nothing of Siegfried or Lohengrin about him; and in Sternberg's films we find, besides the beautiful woman, the athletic young man who has to duck when he passes through a doorway, physically striking like a race horse: Hans Albers in *The Blue Angel*, Gary Cooper in *Morocco*, Victor McLaglen in *Dishonored*, Clive Brook in *Shanghai Express*, Herbert Marshall in *Blonde Venus*. And with the intellectual's typical love for biological perfection, Sternberg directs those robust types, renders them sympathetically, giving them an intelligent appearance, ensures they learn to smile, to sacrifice themselves and resign themselves with discretion. He transfuses into them his own more limpid, livelier blood, without the least coagulation; he makes use of his actors like tools without will, at bottom despising them; he rehearses scrupulously with them right to the subtlest nuance, and before anything else, he takes care to attenuate their gestures according to today's naturalistic style, which cannot displease people of taste.

For the excessive gestures of the theatre, absolutely out of place on the screen, Sternberg substitutes a style of representation which, by giving life to the features, has almost no more need of pantomime, and he entrusts everything to their reality and to their action. Sternberg hates sentimental gesture: and in those cases where he permits it, there is no need to gawp and wave the arms to make the spectator understand what is happening on the screen, because the action is so aptly carried from the interior to the exterior. There comes to mind a little scene, from the days when Sternberg was making his first sound film in Berlin: *The Blue Angel*. This concerned the retaking of a secondary scene: one of the schoolboys very quietly creeps up on Professor Unrat and slips into his pocket the silk drawers of the singer Lola-Lola. The young actor performed the scene as he would have performed it in a hundred other films: he leered slyly and winked to the spectator. When he had played the scene for the first time, Sternberg, who was remaining inconspicuous and calm on his folding chair, spoke with a voice which, weak as he was, made itself heard without difficulty in the middle of all the uproar of the shooting stage, with his accent already slightly tainted with English: 'I want you to give the scene an absolutely serious tone'. And only when the youth had performed the ridiculous scene with the profound gravity of a soldier crawling up to the enemy on all fours did it assume the charm of a particular artlessness.

We need also to remember — to take one example among a hundred — how, in *Dishonored*, the officer who has been recognised as a spy draws from his holster the pistol with which he will commit suicide, at the same time spitting out grape seeds with an expression that is absolutely immobile and almost bored. We need to recall the disquieting effect of that contrast between what is outwardly visible and the internal meaning, in order to understand a characteristic of Sternberg's style. Nevertheless, we soon realise that in those beautiful scenes Sternberg avails himself, so to speak, of the virtues of his defects: a tasteful sobriety that permits him to reduce any pantomime to a cinematic minimum that is, at least when he represents Germanic settings, densely realistic. It is a sobriety that he has acquired at the cost of the diminution of his original vitality. Outbursts of true temperament which are born of an effective participation in the sufferings and the passions of men, the great instincts, have been supplanted by an irritable sensibility. And it is interesting to observe how the detachment of the Austrian intellectual, born of the subtlest form of European sophistication, found in the atmosphere of the American cinema, an attitude toward life which — outwardly — has a great affinity with his own, but which has nevertheless very different roots: the primitive superficiality of the newly-civilised who confuse 'girls' [sic] with women, because they know nothing better, is well-matched with the exponent of a decadent culture that, through weariness and sophistication, quits real women for 'girls'. The two types of man, coming from opposite roads, meet in common endeavour.

However, as has already been mentioned, there exists an important difference. The primitive American of Hollywood ingenuously pretends that the pallid theatrical world, as his actors can evoke it, reflects that profound, eternal passion that he knows only by hearsay. The acute and ingenious European creates on the sets with a sure intuition, unconscious even of the appropriate internal limits, a world in which men of lifeless hearts and mask-like faces deal with human destinies in the tone of a salon. In general, he tactfully avoids giving the illusion of passion, and thus is born a new reality, coherent enough stylistically, but 50 degrees below normal temperature. One receives in this way, as a man's sincere expression, the first — hardly surpassable and uniquely sincere — incarnation of the emotion of life that dominates in American studios, as well as in a decadent world. The inhuman, taking shape, gives way to something that, through its sincerity, becomes almost human. A European completes Hollywood.

The infantile and false figure of the hip-tossing vamp is transformed into the fascinating austerity of a woman attractive for what she lacks. As a variation of the protagonist of Wedekind's *Erdgeist* a Lulu is born — much more superficial, of course — who has become dangerous not so much for her amorality as for her lack of feeling. This is the meaning of the figure of Marlene Dietrich. She could not be called a great artist, and in what she does she competes with the most vivacious and spirited of film actresses. But it needs to be said that here, with the help of an extremely malleable woman, there has been successfully created an unsurpassable incarnation of the type in which Sternberg's American style culminates. For in this case the utter harmony of the body has the effect of exalting the lack of inner vitality and the biological inferiority. It is the glorification of the defective: and the content of all Marlene Dietrich's films is precisely the story of a woman who attracts men precisely by her sphinx-like indifference (a type of woman whose sincere representation in commercial cinema is possible only if she is arrayed in the sequins and feathers of the prostitute). In following the development of Dietrich through the stills from *The Blue Angel* to *Blonde Venus* one sees how she is used to depict this type with ever greater prominence. One sees how the childish exuberance and irrepressible impudence disappear, as she too undergoes the process seen in so many film actresses, of stiffening and slimming; how her cheeks become hollowed out and her eyes sunken (and the reason is not Hollywood's bad cooking).

Between form and content there is no difference; therefore there is nothing to wonder at if the same spirit that expresses in this woman's figure its own uninterest in all the contents of life, at the same time gives rise, in its cinematic form, to a noteworthy disproportion between the means employed and the end to be achieved. The films of Josef von Sternberg, whether as regards shots, lighting, or framing, are not easily surpassable by any director; any one of his images, especially when taken by that ace photographer Lee Garmes, constitutes a miracle of graphic harmony. On the black of the unlighted portion, the few lights stand out like simple reflections. Nevertheless it is obvious that this preciosity does not serve events, but instead is sought as a means of compensating for the poverty of the action — in which the intelligent director gives a good account of himself — with formal values. Moroccan alley, Chinese station, or Russian front: fear of death or lover's jests: everything could enter the precious and sophisticated, decorative style of these images.

The technical means of expression of any art are limited; they become inexhaustible only under the hand of genius. From white to black there is no great distance; but in a Rembrandt they are the poles of a world, while in a Caravaggio, for instance, they serve only to render more enchanting the rosy body of a cherub, in such a way that the light loses its power of symbolic expression, and is reduced to a simple, terrestrial optical effect. In an analogous way the art of the perfect craftsman Sternberg exhausts itself in overnourishing the eye, while the spirit languishes.

And this is made obvious above all in the imitators, who do not possess the taste and the moderation of Sternberg. A man like Rouben Mamoulian, certainly gifted, but equally certainly unthinkable without Sternberg and Lubitsch, does not hesitate to deck his films lavishly in blackness; hardly one of his figures goes for a moment to a corner to telephone but a gigantic shadow is already projected on the ceiling. And also the average American directors, in Sternberg's steps, have become veritable noctambulists: producing stuff to compel the film-lover to arm himself with a portable lamp. Sternberg does not commit such outrageous excesses; even here, once more, he makes use of the virtues of his defects. As he urges the actor to temperance, so also he holds within reasonable limits his orgies of the 'pictorial'. And within the image he is exemplary in reducing outward action to just what serves to emphasize his favourite motifs: the psychological finesse of the acting and the effects of decor.

In general, he limits the simple development of the action to brief yet extraordinarily significant images. This permits him to insist on scenes of true, appropriate performance, which often remain entirely static. One sees in the work an intelligence in the command of the maximum richness of means for the realisation of its capacities, and which lacks only one thing: an object worth the trouble. Whether his own fault or that of someone else, it is difficult, or perhaps pointless, to establish.

(translated by Peter Baxter)

AENEAS MACKENZIE

Leonardo
of the Lenses

(originally published in Life and Letters Today, *Vol. 14, No. 2 (Spring, 1936),
pp. 170–5)*

In any discussion of Hollywood motion-picture direction, the name of
Josef von Sternberg must come either first or last. And it matters not
which, because what distinguishes him is his method. Certainly, as to his
ranking in the profession, there can be no question: he stands with — if
apart from — Ernst Lubitsch and Rouben Mamoulian in a leadership of
American cinema. But so individual is his conception of the medium,
and so distinctive is his resulting technique, that to compare him with
any other director is impossible.

It is a preposterous circumstance that nothing should be published in
the United States on the subject of the film save estimates by literary
minds as to the purely literary values of what is in no true sense a literary
medium. Indeed there can be but small doubt that cinema has suffered
more from the absence of an intelligent body of criticism than from any of
the other factors which have combined to stultify its development here in
Hollywood. Achievement after achievement, beyond the range of any
other medium, has escaped the observation of superciliously superior
critics, who, even at this late date, continue under the delusion that
dramatics, dialogue and *décor* — plus photography! — constitute the sum
total of a motion picture.

Thus, when von Sternberg made his oft-quoted remark, 'I have
nothing to learn from Europe', it was instantly seized upon as an
example of movie megalomania. Yet, in saying this, he was merely
stating a fact which was patently obvious to any one with the knowledge
of what direction implies. There was nothing then, as there is nothing
now in any other school of cinema — save the Marxian dialectic, of
course — which von Sternberg could adopt into his method without
destroying it utterly.

Unquestionably that method has its roots in a deep regard for painting
as a fine art. To know anything about it, to understand what he is
attempting to do, one must first appreciate that he imposes the limitation
of the visual upon himself: he refuses to obtain any effect whatsoever save

42

by means of pictorial composition. That is the fundamental distinction between von Sternberg and all other directors. Stage acting he declines, cinema in its conventional aspect he despises as mere mechanics, and dialogue he employs primarily for its value as integrated sound. The screen is his medium — not the camera. His purpose is to reveal the emotional significance of a subject by means of a series of magnificent canvases.

Any such process in itself, of course, would be purely illustrative, and totally impractical because of its static nature. Nevertheless, a successful von Sternberg film is completely dynamic. The movement of a play on the stage (or of a stage play on the screen) is obtained by means of the literary principle of dramatic impulsion, the so-called *filmic motion* of cinema is induced by a regulation of the length and succession of its individual scenes, and the progression of the factory-made 'movie' is procured by the introduction of entertaining irrelevancies; yet, all of these momenta are denied to von Sternberg by the very nature of what he is attempting to accomplish.

In lieu of them he relies upon long and elaborate shots, each of which is developed internally — by camera movement and dramatic lighting — to a point where it detonates into shock, surprise, or startling beauty. And it is by means of this Ford-like internal combustion that a von Sternberg film progresses in audience-interest; before the effect of one emotional percussion has subsided, the next is underway. Consequently, the story does not move his picture; it is his picture which moves the story.

His camera travels (usually opens) *within the scene* to reveal sectional designs, each representing a tonal facet of the whole in point or counterpoint, and finally unveils the dynamic highlight in an established relationship to all of its component elements. Every iota of material, whether animate or inanimate, is thus brought to one focal point of pure emotion. In reality the technique is a form of cinema in suspension, with the internal movement of a picture dependent on percussions, and with camera mobility substituted for the 'cutting' process of montage.[1]

In dramatic direction, in the handling of the players themselves, the entire technique of stage acting is discarded by von Sternberg. What he attempts to obtain on the screen is abstract human emotion in place of its theatrical indications. And his ability to procure it needs no greater tribute than the mention of an unforgettable fade-out on Marlene Dietrich as she stood, rebuffed, behind Clive Brook's chair on the observation platform of the Shanghai Express. A fade-out on her face against the background of a sable collar: without acting, without cinema, and without a spoken word, von Sternberg revealed the Shanghai Lily's struggle against an inevitable fate, her débâcle, and her spiritual self-justification of it, in fifty feet of film.

It has remained for this mode of direction to demonstrate that the

43

high-light of visual significance in a scene is seldom or ever its literary point of dramatic conflict. But that, no doubt, is the reason why a charge of 'throwing away situations' is so frequently preferred against von Sternberg by theatrical critics, who become indignant when his players are not permitted to re-enact an already established crisis by the conventional forensic process.

The fabrication of the factory-made movie, which constitutes about ninety-five per cent of Hollywood's output, commences with the construction of a framework of dialogue upon which the picture is subsequently assembled. In these illustrated broadcasts it is dialogue which determines the shots, and not shots which determine the dialogue. But dialogue is, chronologically, the final consideration with von Sternberg, and his principal effort — since the significance of his scene is already in being — is to integrate it with the visual elements he has employed. Thus, for example, in the train sequences of *Shanghai Express* he utilized conversation quite successfully to sustain an effect of motion. You may recall how his players read their lines in monotonous running monotones against an intervening accompaniment of clicking wheels.

In the face of actual results there can be no very valid objections either to von Sternberg's conception of his medium or the resulting technique. They comprise a logical process, though one not without pronounced limitations — as will be shown — when certain varieties of subject matter are encountered. But it does involve the very practical consideration that only an individual of unusual creative endowment can employ it with the slightest hope of success. And for that reason von Sternberg's influence on his Hollywood contemporaries has been consistently deplorable — though Paramount's Mitchell Leisen seemed able to rationalize it somewhat to his requirements in *Cradle Song* and *Death Takes a Holiday*.

However, that von Sternberg himself is unusual can hardly be gainsaid. Although the conventional beauty of his compositions may at times be touched by others, in the sustaining of them throughout an entire film he knows few peers. Yet the creative demand on him is much greater than on any of his confrères. Bear in mind that each of his shots is developed on the screen to its point of percussion, while those of other directors have an emotional basis laid for their impact by a dramatic or cinematic process. Only a remarkable degree of resourcefulness in visual ideology, backed by an integrity of pictorial composition, could have enabled him to survive.

Consider for a moment the wedding sequence from *Scarlet Empress*, with its great diagonal plane of lighted candles into which the heads and shoulders of little groups of clergy were spotted [*sic*] — flush with the background — to form a mosaic amid the swaying flames. Here is a perfect example of that purely visual ideology which is von Sternberg's out-striking characteristic as a screen artist. No doubt on reflection it will

44

be easy enough to estimate why this composition conveyed the instant *sense* of inhuman religious observantism to the audience, but to deduce the mental process by which it was conceived in the first instance may prove somewhat more of an enigma.

Although it is far from being his outstanding achievement as an entity, perhaps no single film so well exemplifies the visual approach and spacious range of von Sternberg's direction as *Scarlet Empress*. And for that reason it may be of interest to consider it in some detail. His purpose in patterning this film was to capture the emotional significance of an historic situation in the dual perspective of History itself; by revealing the action and its motivating background in the light of contemporary time. In tempo the picture was designed to follow a series of musical forms — prelude, rondo, scherzo, etc. — and to climax in an intense crescendo movement with the thundering squadrons which swept the young Tsarina from the Cathedral of Kazan to the steps of the Romanoff throne.

An opening sequence revealed the homespun sophistries of the Lutheran little province of Anhalt-Zerbst, resting contentedly in its Rotarian assurance that everything worked for the best in the best of all possible worlds. One glimpsed the future empress being educated there to a conviction that Justice, Chastity, and Faith in Providence were the sole essential attributes of sovereignty. And this first phase of the film thereupon disclosed, with an ironic shot (in the manner of a Victorian steel engraving) which turned the entire court of the preposterous little principality into stuffed shirts and dressmaker's dummies.

From this background the fragrant young Catherine then emerged, in a characterization established to the most minute detail by a few frames of film which showed her descending a winding stairway. What could have been more virginal, convincing, or complete than her significance as an individual in the shot? But in the succeeding sequence of her meeting with the Russian envoy, every element of sound-cinema had been unified to reveal the girl's entire intellectual resources crumbling into chaos at her first contact with Reality! Here von Sternberg made demands upon his star which could not have been met by an actress of the stage school, and his subtle employment of dialogue was in direct antithesis to every theatrical principle: in order to emphasize Catherine's dazed incredulity at the incredible individual who confronted her, the supporting players were instructed to 'jump' the envoy's lines in an astonishing series of unaccentuated exchanges. It is superfluous to suggest that the conceiving and sustaining of such scenes as these bear no closer relation to the childish, reproductive processes of commercial direction than does cinema to the daguerreotype.

But at this point in the picture there followed the scherzo, a swift-flying sleigh sequence, designed to whirl the audience as well as Catherine from the placid conventionality of her home in Anhalt-Zerbst to the terrors of the palace at St. Petersberg. It was the first of two sequences (the other being the cavalry-ride finale) in which the director attempted to rely upon intense visible motion for the impulsion of the film. And each of them proved a problem with which his method could not cope. Readers of Eisenstein and Pudofkin need not be reminded that to capture the emotional significance of action on a screen, such action must be arrested, broken up, and imparted as internal movement to the picture itself by means of a montage process. Here however, and for obvious reasons, camera mobility proved inadequate to von Sternberg as a substitute for cutting. He could neither develop these scenes satisfactorily nor achieve the essential percussion effects. Nevertheless, his effort to obtain the latter was ingenious. It consisted in shooting the action while the same was being cramped by a change in its direction — by closing-up on the sleighs or the squadrons as they turned through an angle of ninety degrees. This, of course, was in accordance with the basic cinema-principle of arresting the motion, and one is tempted to speculate upon what might have been accomplished with the aid of an ultra-rapid camera at such instants. But it would have been wiser had the two sequences been avoided altogether. Their net result was to bring the film to a dead stop at the very points where velocity was essential to its success.

It is obvious that von Sternberg's real weakness as a director lies in his sense of literary discrimination. Yet, occasionally he can surmount it in a surprising manner, and the central situation of *Scarlet Empress* revealed him at his best in that regard. Despite the welter of drunkenness, lust, and slavering insanity in which Catherine found herself on arriving at St. Petersberg, it was the attitude of her future subjects toward religion which the director saw as the most devastating realization of all to the innocent young Protestant princess. Only a few years previously, at the ukase of Peter the Great, they had emerged overnight from an Oriental barbarism to assume the trappings of Western civilization and Western religion. But in the latter it was crucifixion, blood-atonement, and maceration which these Slavic sadists and Mongol masochists had seen and seized upon as Orthodox Greek Catholicism. They worshipped pain at the court of Muscovy in 1745. In whatever direction Catherine might turn, she would find herself confronted by an instinct of disinterested viciousness which would regard her fate as an evidence of divine will.

Therein lay the core of the picture. That Catherine exploited her own physical person as a means to survive and triumph over her individual circumstances was mere episode to von Sternberg — literature, which a cameraman could set up and reproduce at will. And he had no intention of uncovering that episode in any manner short of materializing its complete emotional inducement as well. To do this, he borrowed a somewhat startling device from a more impressionistic realm of expression: the hundreds of distorted ecclesiastical figures, those writhing saints in orgasmic anguishes of martyrdom, which appeared everywhere throughout the palace sequences of the picture.

Contrary to the opinions of our literary critics, this statuary had no symbolic significance, and appeared in the film for no other purpose than to be seen. Like the El Greco distortions which probably inspired their employment, the purpose of the pieces was to suggest the aura of a mutilating religious asceticism through which the action of the picture would appear. They were designed to recreate in the audience a *sense* of that obscene and menacing overtone from which Catherine could not have escaped for an instant during the earlier period of her existence at the Russian court. Note that it was not necessary for a spectator to know anything concerning either the artistic significance of the distortions themselves or the historical circumstances which induced their employment. The audience reflex desired was obtained and controlled through the simple process of seeing. As Catherine began to solve the problem of her personal security, the emotional effect of the device was progressively permitted to subside: although the statues still remained in view, the camera no longer led the eye to them or centered upon individual pieces; till, finally, the audience — like the empress — was released from an oppression and left free to react with her to the film's climactic episode in her own stirring spirit.

It may fall to my lot at some later date to define the three distinct fields of direction, as we know it here and to identify the leading figures in each of them, with their achievements. But from these von Sternberg stands apart.

Note

1. Because of the importance of this mobility, von Sternberg in shooting usually relies upon the camera boom, a device which permits entry into a scene in any plane, for any detail, without dismembering the composition. And to see this dinosaur-like monster followed through the darkness of a sound-stage by a shambling giraffe with a microphone face is one of the most vivid impressions that Hollywood can afford a visitor.

Saint Janet

(originally published in Cahiers du Cinéma, *No. 86 (August 1958), pp. 51–3)*

Here is what *Jet Pilot* is not. Once and for all let's have done with the endless legends regarding it: the seven years of editing and thinking about editing, the continuity-shots filmed two years ago by this *'pauvre Jules'*, still awaiting inclusion. For this film, which on paper benefitted from those questionable advantages of its mysteriousness, a film Sternbergian only in spite of itself, avowedly a hybrid, and therefore an impersonal failure, stands revealed on the contrary as a poetic essay marked by sincerity and serenity, free of all the slag that mars commercial Hollywood undertakings.

Anti-red propaganda? Because it was part of the assignment, the propaganda seems to me quite external to the film, despite certain moments of lovely humour. The problem is not tackled: it is not Uncle Joe's communism that is ridiculed, but Slavic chauvinism, not so much the individual Russian as the most traditional folklore. Certainly the moralist has no right to be sarcastic except with what has no internal consistency. Negative characters are reduced to puppets, but here it is by simple omission and lack of interest rather than by conscious effort. Nevertheless, the intentions if not the realisation of the film are directly related to its very nexus.

To quote the director:

We soon are sick and tired of what is useful alone. The Russian experiment is not over yet, nor is it confined to Russia. There was a good reason for wanting to abolish art. Art creates beauty, and beauty is disturbing to those who wish to contemplate ugliness. René Fülöp-Miller told me that Lenin could not listen to music. Listen to Lenin: *But I can't often listen to music, it goes against the grain of my nerves. I would like to talk sweet nothings and fondle the heads of these people who can create such beauty in the midst of a dirty hell. But today is not the time to fondle the heads of human beings; today their skulls must be split, pitilessly — though the battle against force is our last ideal — a difficult task.*

Men who create beauty do not split heads pitilessly, and the creation of beauty is not quite so easy as murder. Expressed in various ways, beauty is synonymous with our longing to escape from the commonplace. It is the period of peace, in which we gather our strength for the conflict of life, and it is the reason for such conflict. All we fight for is to make life beautiful. But in fighting for beauty we must distinguish between those who fight to make their own life beautiful and those who fight to make the lives of others beautiful. Force beauty in others and you're in trouble. Each man has his own seventh heaven. But beauty does not force, it does not clamour — it releases. The artist and the reformer are non-identical. You can teach others to see, but you cannot overcome resistance to beauty with bodily violence or any other kind of violence.[1]

It is indeed remarkable that the wiles of Furthman and Sternberg should be of the same style, that they should be applied to political or philosophical significance, or to eroticism. It seems that erotic verve is indissociable from contempt for all community, from frantic exaltation of individuality in the furtherance of traditional social and moral principles. Kyrou too often forgets this. This is the way it is with the two summits of the genre: *Jet Pilot* and *The Fountainhead*.

Is the subject of this reactionary film jet propulsion and its importance in the realm of aeronautics? No, for Sternberg is not in the least interested in technology. On that level, even going back eight years, *Jet Pilot* seems out of touch. But if it is expressly superseded by more serious studies of the question, which can be found in the works of Pollen H. Drake and Jean Volpert, it nevertheless overtakes them on the side of aesthetics. If this lag has increased with the years — and with it the rational for the successive tamperings — today it remains nonetheless the most beautiful of aviation films. Why? Because, in a way, the spectacle is an extension of the human factor. It shows us, by concrete signs which have nothing of the symbolic about them, but draw their meaning from that art of the sign, of the bold sketch so dear to our time and so rich in aesthetic possibilities, the very expression of emotions; something at which so many ambitious cineastes, such as Vadim, consistently fail. Thus those shots where the two aircraft twist around one another, coo gently to each other, where the meeting of the planes leads to their slow, magnetic liaison, where the tailpipe of the hero's airplane spews smoke toward the heroine's. We shouldn't be surprised by these subtleties; Jules Furthman, a scenarist for Hawks and Hawksian himself, is without a doubt the best screenwriter that Hollywood has seen, and a specialist in the question. It was he who got underway the canny project of *The Outlaw*.

The same spirit informs even the purely sentimental scenes: the dialogue mixes the frivolous and the serious, suggestiveness and purity of sentiments, in an admirable balance of beauty, of frankness, and of truth. Take as an example the couple in Palm Springs by moonlight.

But is it really true that the spectacle has no value in itself? This is without doubt the key to the success of *Jet Pilot* . . . we admire the beauty of the frolics of the two aircraft, but also their unreality. And, exceptionally for the American cinema, it is the unreality of the spectacle here that makes the film more spectacular yet. This is a work of old age, in which, as in every art that has arrived at maturity, we find inseparably united the detached and easy tone of the author in the face of reality, and also the realist inspiration, which can reveal to us the rough charm of a gesture or a gait.

Jet Pilot is a film on and for Janet Leigh. But already certain voices have asked what there is to justify Sternberg's infatuation for Janet, this sleek and desirable doll without personality. She is more evocative of the cover-girls of 1958 than the exceptional women of the Marlene Dietrich type who excited the young Sternberg. Janet Leigh is beautiful in herself, but she lacks, if I dare express it this way, that spice of femininity, that '+x=infinity' that is generally related to some physical defect, a nose askew, a mouth too wide, or chin too large, related to a fault with respect to the canons of aesthetics, which opens the way to a kind of sublimeness, and to the establishment of a more direct contact with the spectator. *The Black Shield of Falworth* and *Pete Kelly's Blues* disappointed us a little in this regard, and we shall have to await some Wellesian lighting for the lack to be filled. Time alone, with the help of genius, will be able to make that necessary fault appear.

Now, with the help of his power of invention alone, Sternberg sometimes arrives at an identical result. His evolution explains the variations of his inspiration. In the thirties he was marked by aestheticism and much less sensitive to the subterfuges needed in directing actors; this is why we are so bored when watching *Blonde Venus*. Now, to a pure *metteur en scène,* Janet Leigh offers many more resources, resources which have the advantage of always presenting themselves as potential, and as exciting to invention, than Marlene, a strong personality, always self-consistent. Sternberg had only to costume her, and fold his arms. Here, however, he can work on his actress, and give her any personality he desires; he is even obliged to, for a Janet Leigh left to herself and endlessly immobile, would be no more than one pretty girl among so many others, like Terry Moore, who has not yet found her *metteur en scène.* He has lost none of his genius for costume (rather to the contrary; think of the golden blouse, the red trousers with the lightning fasteners on the sides, already anticipating the parachute-skirts of *Anatahan*); and he has achieved the genius of the cineaste.

She smiles, eats, and above all moves, moves with a grace that Sternberg was able to make sublime: the automatic toss of her hair, plays of position on the beds (always different), of lips, of gaits (her rhythmic and determined dash to the airplane; her pretty duck-like stride during the couple's argument).

Sternberg's technique, still very much that of the silent cinema, with its predominance of close-ups, plays its cards on effects. The sureness of his touch is happily allied to the delicacy of the general tone, and to the *objective charm* emanating from it.

The last shot, of the cigarette-girl's legs, tilts up toward Janet Leigh's face. Let us therefore praise filmmakers who, in their contempt for the false values of the scenario, of good taste, of unity of tone and of reason, preserve a little of that lunatic genius that takes the liberty of a pure joke of *mise en scène*, something that on paper seems absolutely gratuitous and devoid of sense. Sternberg is enjoying himself. It is therefore a serious matter.

(translated by Peter Baxter)

Note

1. Josef von Sternberg, 'More Light', *Sight and Sound*, Vol. 25, No. 2 (Autumn 1955), p. 74.

The von Sternberg Principle

(originally published in Esquire, *Vol. 60, No. 4 (October 1963), pp. 80–97, 172)*

Overtly, these charming photographs of the personable young women thus presented speak for themselves, but then also for the skill of the craftsman whose purpose it was to make a likeness memorable. Without expert knowledge of what passes for glamor, I do have some slight familiarity with its dynamics.

To many of my colleagues and to their admirers, 'glamor' has almost become a dirty word. Their battle cry is 'Down to Earth!' as if reducing everything to the status of a worm were an admirable achievement. This, with the help of 'the angry young men', has practically succeeded in eliminating grace and charm from the cultural pattern of our day. It has induced a current vogue of drabness which has almost become fashionable, and has been acclaimed to be so desirable that unless a female makes herself entirely unattractive it cannot be said of her that she did her best to improve her appearance.

Occasionally the panoply of glamor applied to all and sundry becomes cloying and should be subjected to discipline. But discipline is one thing, and being asked in its name to admire an ash can is another. Also I must assume some responsibility for this unforeseen turn of events, for in one of my earlier films I had Miss Dietrich dress in well-cut trousers without fully considering the frightful influence she exerted on others.

In photography, glamor is found in the fusion of the model with the photographer's vision. Glamor functions only on the viewer: the subject itself does not come under its own spell.

Although women love to be photographed in every conceivable position, there are some poses they are asked to hold, apparently with effortless nonchalance, which are not only incomprehensible to them but which are tantamount to being strung on a rack. I recall Marlene's complaints, while she submitted to fitting into my vision of her, that for nothing in the world would she care to undergo such torment as she thought was being inflicted in her. She did not object to her transformation, but neither did she relish it. Of course, in her case the glamor had to be maintained in motion, not on being made to appear ravishing in a few posed photographs. It is quite simple to produce a glamorous impression while holding still; movement contains a thousand and one pitfalls to destroy the enchantment. Curiously enough the power of glamor in a photograph consists of the idealized image promising movement, with no disturbing awkwardness or restraint; it induces an evocation of an image of sexual surrender. One should not go too deeply into this topic, into the erotic core of the meaning of glamor; some startling conclusions might emerge, although in this Age of Freud it may not be possible to startle anyone.

Glamor is the quality of being provocative, tantalizing, entrancing, fascinating, ravishing and bewitching, all these implying vibrating and twisting the beholder's emotional wiring. Glamor can also produce, though this is rare, a purely aesthetic satisfaction, divorced from all primitive impulse, by first draining the blood from your body.

Once a woman has been presented in such a way as to weave this potent spell, no denaturized and deglamorized contact with the original of this skillful effigy can wipe out the fraudulent image. You may hereafter look for it in vain, but look for it you will. In a sense, the photographer, in garlanding a female with charm and qualities not her own, perpetrates a fraud. For this creature he has constructed does not exist in reality.

It is not my intention to diminish the stature of womanhood, for there is nothing on earth that is more graceful and attractive than a female in bloom. Nature did a lot of experimenting before it arrived at a perfect version. But man is not content to value a woman for the extraordinary qualities that took millions of years to flower, and will often favor an image that has qualities that took no longer than the split second that transfers the real thing into a black box to become an illusion.

There are styles in glamor, as in everything else; one year glamor is partial to plump ladies in tights and on a bicycle, as in the early daguerreotypes; another year it embraces inflated bosoms, gartered legs, veils, and extravagant hats, features rapturous expressions, angelic eyes, saccharine nudes of the pinup syndrome, and now documentary blackness, but one — and the principal — facet of glamor never changes: it promises something it cannot deliver.

Glamor, as was indicated before, affects the spectator much as a hungry dog may be affected by the sight of a juicy bone in a butcher's window. Glamor is an elastic concept, composed of a play of fluid values, of imponderables artfully arranged in a spiritual space, a visual stimulant achieved by flummery. The craftsman who manipulates the subject with little concern for its welfare and bounces light on it to capture a fleeting moment is responsible for the glamor of a photograph, not the object in front of the lens.

Glamor in a photograph is the treatment of surface — a surface that is not even skin deep: it is only as deep as the paper which produces the image. In case the point has not yet been made clear: inner beauty and outer beauty do not have the same address.

It has been suggested that glamor is a lost art. I don't believe that it ever was a common commodity that had a beginning and an end. It is not an invention that began with photography. Legends of glamor go deep into history. To mention a few, there was Helen who launched a thousand ships, Phryne who befuddled a jury, Cleopatra of the rolled up carpet, and the more recent Duse who chose to grovel at the feet of d'Annunzio: the list of glamorous women is legion. One must, of course, take into consideration that glamor of a high order cannot be achieved without a formidable personality to back it up. A nude on a calendar no matter how alluring, is one in a thousand until it become identified with the personality of Marilyn Monroe.

The two most popular representatives of glamor in the earlier days of the motion picture, before the medium became a visual skeleton clattering with voices, were Garbo and Valentino. As far as Valentino is concerned, the less said the better; his antics bordered on the ridiculous. But the so-called glamorous image of Garbo has displayed a remarkable persistency. Brought from Sweden and tutored by a master craftsman, Mauritz Stiller, she succeeded in making an entire world aware of her grace and personality. Were her image, which is still glamorous, analyzed objectively, it would reveal a languorous, almost anemic appearance, a husky, almost male, voice and a luminous pair of tragic eyes that looked within rather than at what was to be seen. But glamor is difficult to see objectively. Garbo's image had an impact not only on most men, but on practically every woman. She did not consider herself glamorous — far from it — but the very mention of her name could produce ecstasy in other women.

That she thus affected others of her sex is worth noting, for one would normally assume that glamor in a woman is intended to arouse only the male. In every country thousands of women were fascinated and deeply affected by her image, and tried to imitate her, if possible. But what is it that attracts women to a glamorous female? I can only venture a guess. Either they suffer from the confusion of not knowing whether they are essentially male or female, or they are thrilled that one of their own sex achieved the ultimate in sexual attractiveness. Or, maybe, as they know that no female could actually look so perfectly feminine in reality, it gives them hope that with the aid of cosmetics, beauty parlours and hairdressers, and under favorable light conditions, they can also manage an appearance that might help to make a lasting impression.

Be that as it may, with very few exceptions, glamor is not created by a woman desirable as she might temporarily be, but by a craftsman with superb control, who can manipulate lights, camera, his chosen subject and his perceptiveness until an aggregate is achieved that can no longer be broken down into any of the components that have been so skillfully

54

fused. Technically, glamor consists of the chiaroscuro, the play of light on the landscape of the face, the effect of the background, the composition, the planting of mysterious shadows in the eyes to conceal the vacancy, the aura of the hair, and to capture all this in a fleeting moment of grace.

Exceptional photographs of human beings are not common, not so much because of the scarcity of exceptional human beings (personally, I think that there are few human beings that are not exceptional), but because there are few exceptional directors and photographers. Most photographers are content to capture what is before the glass eye with the hope that the negative is properly exposed, and, made fidgety by an awkward instrument, they may not be able to restrain their impulse to click the shutter whenever the model holds still long enough while not having a bored expression. Though even this result can be improved in the postmortem of the darkroom by manipulation of the negative and print, it takes more than technical proficiency to endow a subject with the superb quality of glamor.

I would not wish to rate it too highly, nor do I care to diminish its importance in adding luster to what otherwise might remain unnoticed. Glamor is an ingredient that has its place in all the arts, and is used by everyone within his means who wishes, in Goethe's words, to state: 'Oh, could I but say to the moment — stand still — thou art so beautiful!'

'The von Sternberg Principle' by Josef von Sternberg (October 1963). Reprinted by permission of *Esquire* Magazine. Copyright © 1963 by Esquire, Inc.

Belated Appreciation of V.S.

(originally published in Film Culture, *No. 31 (Winter 1963–64), pp. 4–5)*

People never know why they do what they do. But they have to have explanations for themselves and others.

So Von Sternberg's movies had to have plots even though they already had them inherent in the images. What he did was make movies naturally — he lived in a visual world. The explanations plots he made up out of some logic having nothing to do with the visuals of his films. The explanations were his bragging, his genius pose — the bad stories of his movies. Having nothing to do with what he did, (& did well) the *visuals* of his films.

In this country the movie is known by its story. A movie is a story, is as good as its story. Good story — good movie. Unusual story — unusual movie, etc. Nobody questions this. It is accepted on all levels, even 'the film is a visual medium' levels by its being held that the visuals are written first and then breathed into life by a great cameraman, director. In this country the blind go to the movies. There is almost no film an experienced & perceptive blind man couldn't enjoy. This is true. I was a B'way barker once & was approached by a blind man! The B.M. was right — there must be others! The manager, nobody thought it strange — at the time I didn't — and don't now. I do think it strange that nobody uses their eyes. Occasionally a director will put in a 'touch' — that can't be explained with words, needn't be, and this is always telling. But the literature of the film, its words, trite, necessarily so, for they are always doing something they shouldn't have to do, they are forced into triteness because they shouldn't be there at all — they should be in novels, anecdotes, conversations, etc. — (NO, movies are not conversations — why should they be so limited!) Music belongs, film is rhythm, so is music — if dialogue could be seen as rhythm it would belong. But just rhythm — not the printed page.

I don't think V.S. knew that words were in his way, but he felt it — neglected them, let them be corny & ridiculous, let them run to travesty — and he invested his images with all the care he rightfully denied the words. And he achieved the richest, most alive, most right images of the world's cinema — in company with men like Von Stroheim, the genius of *Zéro de Conduite*, early Lang & that limited company — Ron Rice today.

His expression was of the erotic realm — the neurotic gothic deviated sex-colored world and it was a turning inside out of himself and magnificent. You had to use your eyes to know this though because the sound track babbled inanities — it alledged[1] Dietrich was an honest jewel thief, noble floosie, fallen woman etc., to cover up the visuals. In the visuals she was none of those. She was V.S. himself. A flaming neurotic — nothing more nothing less — no need to know she was rich, poor, innocent, guilty etc. Your eye if you could use it told you more interesting things (facts?) than those. Dietrich was his visual projection — a brilliant transvestite in a world of delerious unreal adventures. Thrilled by his/her own movement — by superb taste in light, costumery, textures, movement, subject and camera, subject/camera/revealing faces — in fact all revelation but *visual* revelation. An example of how visual information informs. The script says Count so and so (in *Devil is a Woman)* is a weak character. The plot piles up situation after situation — but needlessly — Sternberg graphically illustrates this by using a tired actor giving a bad performance. If his hero is a phoney for the purposes of the story, V.S. casts an actory actor in the part & leads him into hammy performance. Which comes to the acting in V.S. films. He got his effects directly through the eye. If the woman is deceptive he would *not* get Dietrich to give a great (in other words the convention of good acting wherein maximum craft conveys truthfulness) perf. of a woman conning. He would let her struggle hopelessly with bad lines she couldn't handle even if she were an actress. He let her acting become as bad as it could become for her. [A bad actor is a rich, unique, idosyncratic, revealing of himself not of the bad script. Select the right bad actor and you can have a visual revelation very appropriate to the complex of ideas and sets of qualities that make up your film. V.S. knew this and used bad acting regularly as a technique for visual revelation (not story telling).] For he was concerned with personal, intuitive, emotional values — values he found within himself — not in a script. With people as their unique selves, not chessmen in a script.

Possibly he might have been afraid of reaction if it were known that this visual fantasy world was really his own mind. He might have deliberately obscured, distracted attention from the shock that might have occured if his creation had been understood through the eye. To close the ears would have thrown the viewer into an undersea, under-conscious, world where the realities were very different from what the script purported. He needn't have worried. As it was no one had that ability to see. He was misunderstood and well understood. Well understood in that his covert world disturbed; Misunderstood in that no one knew why or appreciated the wonder of being disturbed. Misunderstood and done an injustice to in that finally when opinion turned against him it was for the wrong reason: (wrong not because people should not be disturbed) the insipid stories, bad acting, bad dialogue etc. Wrong reasons because they were, to be true to his expression, deliberately bad. Then he was punished — turned out of Hollywood and never again allowed to work. Only frightened people punish. Ostensibly because he had violated good technique. Good technique being used as something people hide behind when they are frightened by something they wouldn't like in themselves therefore is in themselves. And the hypocrisy of good acting, good this, good that — GOOD MOVIES being perpetuated — GOOD EMPTY — BANAL — UNTRUE MOVIES — IMPERSONAL MOVIES.

Note

1. Here and elsewhere we reproduce faithfully the original spelling and punctuation. (ed.)

MARCEL OMS

Josef
von Sternberg

(originally published as 'Anthologie du Cinéma 60', a supplement to L'Avant-scène du Cinéma, *No. 109, December 1970)*

Josef von Sternberg died on December 22, 1969, taking with him his enigma and his myth. All those who met him in the last years of his life, as well as those who tried to get him to talk all through his career, know that Sternberg remained impenetrable, hidden behind his own statue.

Having bowed to his creator's will and played the deceptive game of Hollywood and its system, up until the moment of his death he was constant in perpetuating a character that was proud, disdainful, and somewhat sceptical, greatly reassuring to him, and facilitating his contact with the world of critics.

For several years, despite slight variations, Sternberg always gave journalists the same interview. In Mar del Plata, Paris, London, Los Angeles, or San Sebastian, he asserted and re-asserted that he was the sole creator of his films, the sole 'inventor' of Marlene; he asserted and re-asserted his hatred for actors; he defended himself against proposed interpretations of his works, contenting himself with reducing them to their primary, immediate 'reading'.

With a certain coyness, he gave himself to mystification, peered at his interlocutors, seemed always in control of the situation, manifested a prodigious memory for details, polishing and repolishing the marble in which he had once for all sculpted his effigy for posterity.

Nevertheless, cornered sometimes by some imbecile question, fatigued by cross-examinations, and finally tired of playing, the old man rose up behind the shadow of the former director. Thus one saw him at San Sebastian, in June 1969, violently refuse to discuss politics, to judge the significance of student rebellions, in order to protest, with a sudden irritation that vouchsafed his sincerity: 'I too have known poverty. When I was in Vienna, I skipped meals more often than I took them, eating in the street the crust of bread and the chop that I had in the pocket of my overcoat.'

This monument carried within himself, as each of us does, the rift of adolescence; he was in the camp of the humiliated, of the party of those

59

haunted by their profaned childhood. It is more interesting to approach the man than the glacial character he put forward: the man explains the work, and Sternberg's work commands our attention like a long anguished cry, even if its abundant splendours have too often masked its harrowing simplicity.

THE KEYS OF CHILDHOOD

In my opinion, von Sternberg's creative journey advances in a straight-forward, particularly exemplary way, because it is based on the most common obsessions of all men: the relationship to the father, childhood and play, love, the certitude of death, and the need for eternity.

'My father was an enormously strong man, who often used his strength on me,' writes Josef von Sternberg in his memoirs, *Fun In a Chinese Laundry*. (p. 5.)[1]

One might suggest that it is of him that Sternberg was thinking in choosing George Bancroft for the first (and in my opinion the most personal) part of his work.

> However, I did not consider my early days to be lacking in pleasure. I was born with the fragrance of chestnut blossoms in my nostrils . . . And the first sounds I heard were mingled with the melodies that floated into my crib from the hurdy-gurdies, calliopes and wondrously decorated music boxes . . . in the Prater . . . (p. 6.)

Further on we will see the place of festival in the Sternbergian thematic, the conscious resurgence of the climate of childhood, but also the promise and prefiguration of another universe: one where rapture gives wing to the imagination.

> The event of those tender years, as the age of fourteen approached, was a deep plunge into puppy love. . . . It never entered my mind to touch this fragile vision . . . But a more practical friend of mine with no such apprehensions closed that chapter for me when I caught them one day wrapped around each other. (p. 14.)

The entire structure of Sternberg's relation to Woman is contained in this first disappointment in love, just as the portrait of this adolescent Viennese girl prefigures the future Marlene: 'The Viennese girl of that time had the most graceful posture. . . . She . . . was lithe and alluring, and had a magic formula for both movement and repose. . . . She permitted me to worship her, and in turn she worshipped herself.' (p. 14.)

However, Sternberg's 'revelation' of woman was not given to him only in this idealized form that was apt to be broken by a brutal awakening.

60

'The blue Danube . . . shows its affection for the city that cradled me by making a lazy excursion that touches tiny islands formed by a tidal basin where I learned to swim. On one of these islands I stumbled on a flock of maidens in the raw. But in a flash the lovely nymphs turned into furies . . .' (p. 13.)

Many times, Sternberg returns to the conflict that truly traumatized his adolescence: that of the simple innocent (who liked 'poetry and flowers') with the filth and perversion of females. And also males: 'A kind teacher took me to his home . . .'; 'men pressed themselves against me on crowded streetcars . . .'; 'a much older boy lavished poetry and flowers on me and swore by all that he held sacred that I would be the pivot of his life if I could only understand.' (pp. 13–14.)

All this leads us to Sternberg's last and permanent obsession, which determines all his work, and subtends the behaviour of his characters: poverty. I spoke above of how Sternberg left off the reserve of a dignified old man to return to the tattered phantoms of his youth, out of which have sprung all his lost, humiliated characters, Lena Smith, Blonde Venus, the extras of *The Last Command*, the 'suicide passengers' of *Morocco*, the flotsam of Shanghai, and the scum of Macao.

Without the mud and the filth, of which he was made youthfully aware, Josef Sternberg would never have desired the *von* of self-ennoblement that was his mask, and that many have taken to be his face.

But without this mud and this filth, the poisonous vegetation or the plumed luxuriance of his style could not have grown and flowered. For Josef von Sternberg's whole work has ceaselessly told the story of a net dragging the mud of a port to retrieve human refuse and salvaged souls. All the rest; the streamers and the oleanders, the farandoles and the wooden horses, the proliferation of pasteboard and the feathery downpours, the sophisticated women and the coloured balloons are only the exotic solicitations of an imagination that is raising its sail and setting out to sea.

DIFFICULT BEGINNINGS

Exegesis of Sternberg's work, privileging the period I will call 'Marlenian', often neglects the silent period of which *The Blue Angel* is but the culmination, forgets *An American Tragedy*, and analyses the final phase in terms of the Dietrich myth. Thus are obscured the entire genesis and blossoming forth of a work without which nothing is explained, and especially not the conclusion of a creative career that decided for itself the date and especially the place of its termination: an island lost in the middle of the Pacific, untiringly battered by the gnawing waves of the ocean. From the port of San Pedro, dredged by the crane of *The Salvation Hunters*, the work of Sternberg arrives on the feverish shores of Anatahan, and defines itself as an ample and uneasy meditation on Water. Thus

Marlene is no longer but one variation among others on the fluidity of emotions and the dark inconstancy of the heart, where *'la mer et l'amour ont l'amer pour partage'*. (Marbeuf). . . .

By his own admission, Sternberg was haunted from the age of seven by the world of the sea-port, and its fauna: 'The long train ride and the fourteen-day voyage across the Atlantic have been wiped from my memory, but not so the port of the city of Hamburg. . . . This bedroom in Hamburg, reserved exclusively for transients who had no other choice, was red-brown with evil insects, walls and bed covered with crawling bedbugs.' (p. 9.)

It is in this context of abject filth and lack of self-respect that a child of seven discovers the universe of missed departures, of frustrated escapes, and of sinking into the mire. An image that returns to assault the mature man, in Calcutta: 'In the temple of Kali in Calcutta, I could not avoid seeing a widow who had invented her own form of suttee. Shrouded in white rags of mourning, her face a mask of sorrow, chalked with dried cow-dung, she sat in her own filth. She could tolerate no inferior.' (Sternberg, 'On Life and Film', *Films in Review*, Vol. III, No. 8 (October 1952), p. 385.)

I accord a decisive importance to these debasing contacts of a being with life in determining his ethical future. Indeed, Sternberg experiences the need so to intensify the depiction of a ludic universe where festival attains sacrificial paroxysms because he could see therein the collective phenomenon by which men disguise life through an intoxication of the senses and emotions. The festival is a simulacrum and disguise through the lyric affirmation of a hidden truth better revealed when it is masked.

It is therefore crucial for our knowledge of Sternberg to examine the profound implications of a first film whose central characters are precisely a child who discovers the filth of life and a crane that scoops up the mud of a port.

The whole thematic of *The Salvation Hunters* rests in effect on a symbolic that is somewhat simplistic at first sight, but which in reality is highly revealing of Sternberg's structures. The film tells us the journey of three beings: a strong and muscular man (the image of the father), a young woman of gentle appearance (the mother), and a child of about seven years (the fantasy Josef von Sternberg himself) who, at the price of violent entanglements, including a knife fight, begin to lift themselves out of the original setting in which they are stagnating at the beginning of the film. The symbolic intention of the author is clear, since he avows that his purpose rests on 'three pieces of human flotsam living on a mudbarge . . . and who finish by escaping this milieu after various incidents considered in their poetic aspect.' (Quoted by *Cahiers du Cinéma*, No. 66.)

Moreover, the first image of the film shows us some wreckage floating in the harbour at San Pedro on which a gull stands like a Holy Ghost. On the planks nailed to the window of our heroes' hovel is written in chalk 'Jesus saves us'. Now, in the film's dramaturgy itself, it is the child who is going to play the role of determinant redeemer, who is going to 'save' the others because his purity guarantees redemption.

Tirelessly, the crane scrapes the mud, raises dirt and filth, wreckage and refuse from the bottom of the bay. Thus the proximity of the monstrous engine serves to describe allegorically the human condition, the heart-rending misery of three creatures in search of salvation.

Ferdinand Pinney Earle was not mistaken in writing in December 1924 (in *The Director*, Vol. 1, No. 7): 'It is the first great symbolical picture ever made, and deals in an original manner with the forces that govern human destiny. There are scenes that are like poignant metaphors and similes — scenes that are like eloquent phrases. Its message is tremendous, terrible, beautiful, and charged with an elemental force that is inescapable. It is an unforgettable sermon that burns its text into the brain and leaves one exalted and strangely moved.'

Sternberg liked this text, which he moreover reprinted in his *Fun in a Chinese Laundry* (p. 22). He therefore accepts its tenor and terms, even taking them as his own. This is important because it reveals an ethical stance which his creative work will constantly make more precise: the proximity of people and the setting that explains them, the dialectic of degradation and salvation, the solitude of emotions that finally reveal themselves to one another by way of a mediator.

Not to admit that all Sternberg's sensibility and morality rest on these principles, to neglect his Judaic education, to close one's eyes to the insistence with which scatological obsessions return in his memories, scabrous impressions, and notions of guilt and sin, is to deny oneself exact knowledge of Sternberg's genius.

Sternberg's whole work is nothing but an agonised meditation on the difficulty of living. Without this philosophic assumption, his baroque aesthetic would have been merely superficial.

In 1926, after the unfortunate attempts of *Escape* and *The Masked Bride*, and an aborted project with Mary Pickford *(Backwash)*, Sternberg made one of the most legendary films in the history of the cinema, *The Sea Gull*, also know as *A Woman of the Sea*. We can only dream of this work where woman and sea meet in a single poem. In reading the rare testimonies of those who saw this film in private, our regrets are sharpened: 'It was a strangely beautiful and empty affair — possibly the most beautiful I have ever seen — of net patterns and hair in the wind.' (John Grierson, *Grierson on Documentary*, p. 60.) But the negative of *The Sea Gull* seems to have been destroyed, and there seems to have remained only one copy of the film, belonging to the producer, Charlie Chaplin, who was dissatisfied with the results. Certain people, like Robert Florey, even think that the film 'was too sophisticated for him; there was too much in it that he was incapable of understanding.'

As for Sternberg, questioned on this *black-out* [*sic*], he was content to reply, 'I think the reason must have been purely financial, a matter of taxes.' (*Positif*, No. 35.)

What we do know of this experience sheds light on Sternberg's contribution to cinematic expression. The split between Chaplin and Sternberg marks more than a disagreement between two men; it is the profound conflict between two conceptions of the cinema. The Dickensian sentimentalism of Chaplin rests on a literary heritage that seeks to translate the internal movements of characters by acting alone.

On the other hand, Sternberg had perfectly understood that the spirit proper to the cinema resided in its aptitude for seeing the interconnexions of the outward and the inward, and that its function was to *show* them by the play of light. Indeed, emotions are only variations of intensity in the light of the heart, of which the white expanse of the screen can bear the reflections.

Sternberg's artistic approach consists of this effort to catch (and capture) the intimacy linking a being and his environment; at the limit to attempt to seize the universal rhythm of things 'through forests of symbols'.

What we can make of *The Sea Gull* on the basis of witnesses and their recollections suggests to us that this film was the dialectical complement of *The Salvation Hunters.* In this latter, the sea, imprisoned by a bay that is dirty with mud and refuse, scraped, stirred up, polluted by the agitation of the barge, suggests flight and the open waves. In *The Sea Gull* (filmed in California, on the coast at Monterey), the sea and the wind opened to the horizon, and 'the changing patterns of the sea . . . were themselves used for psychological as well as atmospheric underscoring of the action.' (Herman Weinberg, *Josef von Sternberg,* p. 27.)

Constrained here to simple suppositions, we should nevertheless specify that the completed edifice of Sternberg's work reveals a permanent oscillation between apparent contradictions. There are, for example, at the end of the count, as many humiliated, defeated women as heartless goddesses; as many ridiculous puppets as triumphant heroes: Bancroft can be the gangster Bull Weed *(Underworld)* as well as Nolan the police officer *(The Dragnet)*, just as the cruel Concha Perez *(The Devil is a Woman)* can differ from the unfortunate mother of *Blonde Venus.* Melancholy gives birth to the ideal. . . .

This suggests that Sternberg's universe and his vision of the world rest on a conflict between pitiless experienced reality, and the deliriums of the imagination, each pulling man into himself, and leading him, in the end, to transcend his condition.

Sternberg's cinema — like that of Bunuel — has constantly filmed the 'communicating vessels' of reality that is irreducible to the immediate evidence of the senses and of consciousness.

That, in order to express himself, he has had recourse to the most 'commercial' genres of film spectacle is only an additional confirmation of the suggestion: the popular, 'successful' genres are precisely those which best translate and reflect the imagination of the masses.

COMMUNICATING VESSELS

At 8:45 AM von Sternberg arrived on the set. All the extras lined up. He reviewed them, inspecting them from head to foot. His general staff followed him at a respectful distance. In front of the twenty-first policeman Sternberg stopped, hypnotised the poor man and then, turning toward the technicians, shouted, 'There's a button missing from the tunic of this policeman. I'll not be insulted in this way.' (Robert Florey, *Hollywood, Yesterday and Today.*)

The general and his general staff advance. The eyes of the general are alert; they succeed in dividing their attention between officers and men. He brandishes his stick; a man steps out of the ranks and buttons his jersey.
(*The Last Command*, scene 10, extract from script.)

I was the first to deal with the film machine in *The Last Command*, in which the late Emil Jannings played the part of an extra. . . . Jannings, who had been Commanding General of the Russian Army, is propelled by fate to Hollywood and there chosen from the ranks of the extras to depict his own history. The picture ended with Jannings driven mad and dying in the belief that he was once more in real command.' (Sternberg, 'Acting in Film and Theatre'.)

The intentional juxtaposition of these three texts makes it apparent that with *The Last Command* Josef von Sternberg revealed the compensating relations between poignant reality and the illusions of artistic creation.

From his own humble experience in the studios, Sternberg drew the background on which his film unrolled. A renowned director (William Powell) chooses from a pile of photographs that of a prospective bit-player, the ex-tsarist general Sergius Alexander (Emil Jannings). They summon the old man, put him in a uniform on which he himself hangs a medal, a souvenir of his past glory. Of the time when he served the tsar . . .

For our part, we enter into the remembrance of things past. Alexander, ten years earlier, during the Revolution of 1917, barely escaped death by firing squad, saved by Natascha Dobrova, the very woman who, though assigned to assassinate him, fell in love with her victim while sharing his life and patriotism.

In the confused days of the insurrection, the train of the general is stopped by the howling mob and Natascha saves her lover by abandoning herself to the bestial embrace of a drunken 'revolutionary'. Alexander leaps from the train just in time to see it plunge from a bridge in the distance, to be swallowed by the ice, and destroyed.

Having returned to the reality of the present, Alexander listens to the instructions of the director, who is none other than the former 'red' agitator, Natascha's confederate. The scene to be shot unfolds, it too being set during the Revolution. Suddenly, for Alexander, the cue of an actor re-awakens the officer's reflex. His reason wavers and, taking fiction for reality, he once more becomes the general of other days, brandishes his sabre to lead his last charge in a sublime *crise de folie*, then collapses. As he lies dead, the Cross of the Order of St. George shines on his chest.

The scenario of *The Last Command* is — I hope it has been realised — completely mad. At the level of ideas alone, it is impossible to maintain that Sternberg could have made a political work of it: like so many others, he swallowed the Hollywood commonplaces of hostility to the events of October (as had for example a year earlier, Cecil B. De Mille with *The Volga Boatman*).

Quite on the contrary, *The Last Command* is a flamboyant melodrama where Evelyn Brent, waving the standard of the Revolution, draws a shouting mob after her, commits treason for the sake of love, and before she can go to the limits of dishonour, disappears in an apocalypse of snow, fire, and ice; where Emil Jannings, tottering in the vanguard, relives the pathetic calvary of his decrepitude before being conquered once again by madness; where sumptuous palaces conceal plots of death, and the mirrors reflect the sensuous dresses of ambiguous heroines . . .

There is much to say on the subject of Sternberg's taste for melodrama and his fondness for sacrificial victims.

Melodrama, by its constant repercussions, permits moving back the limits of the possible by moving back the boundaries of verisimilitude. At the same time, it gives free rein to the powers of invention. In my opinion the meaning and the flavour of melodrama are related to properties of the imagination, because melodrama permits everything, or even better, it makes everything possible. Simultaneously, by a complementary movement, to the same extent that it ensnares characters in the pitiable condition of an exaggerated fatality, it sets up a great potential for escape.

I need no more evidence than that extraordinary project for Sternberg to make *Backwash* with Mary Pickford; 'it concerned a blind girl and a deaf-mute, the subject to be visualized through the eyes of a girl who had never been able to see.' (*Fun in a Chinese Laundry*, p. 207.) Indeed, *Backwash* could have been the film of the absolute imagination, which no longer being occupied by the evidence of the senses, reconstitutes the form of things, and unaware of appearances, apprehends the essence of the world.

Melodramatic plots have an identical function with regard to artist and spectator. For an ordinary spectator, the excesses of the melodrama fill a desire for dream, play the role of compensating for the exceptional that never happens in banal, daily life. 'The average human being', writes Josef von Sternberg, 'lives behind an impenetrable veil and will disclose his deep emotions only in a crisis which robs him of control.' (*Fun in a Chinese Laundry*, p. 56.)

Film plays this role of crisis for the spectator.

For the creator, the situation is different. For Sternberg, the meanderings of the melodrama are the convulsions of a baroque sensibility, and the deliriums of the scenario serve his taste for the impossible.

The spectator being 'fixed' (as the bull is 'fixed' for the killing, squared for the thrust), Sternberg can with impunity abandon himself to his internal spectacles, and externalize them without fear. . . .

Life undoes, smashes, and disperses the impressions of childhood: the ordinary man dies of it; the artist alone, accepting his schizoid vision of the world, can retrieve the lost paradise of unscathed sensations. More than any other, the cinematic creator — this demiurge of a surreality that is capable of illusion since it resembles immediate reality — permits his clients free access to their infancy, promise of the future, because it is a port opening onto the high seas of the dream.

Fully aware that his craft is for him the place where infancy and mature age cease being perceived contradictorily, Sternberg can write, in evocation of his Viennese games and discoveries: 'In another phase of my life, parts of the impression it made on me were passed on to others.' (*Fun in a Chinese Laundry*, p. 8.)

For Sternberg was able to discover more than the cinema's possibilities of expression, the virtualities of a language susceptible of finally achieving universal communication by expresssion of the real and the possible, of the sensible and of talent: 'the camera . . . could be moved, it could look down on its subject, aim up to capture it, bring it close or push it away, it could reveal or conceal it at will, impose a tempo, and add a thousand variables in its endless and unlimited play with light and darkness.' (p. 219.)

For him, the discovery and the practice of sound will only amplify this filmic vocation for liberating the powers of the dream: 'It had brought into what was seen another world, a world that stimulated the imagination beyond the content of what the frame of the camera had shown. . . . Sound had to counterpoint or compensate the image, add to it — not subtract from it . . . Sound was realistic, the camera was not.' (p. 219.)

In the same way that he has illuminated the existential universe by extending it through the filmic universe, Sternberg charges sound with a new vocation: that of *stating* the real, while the image invites evasion. Thus obliging the spectator to participate in the film, urged by all his senses to the illusion of living.

Concern better to describe the meaning of creative structures in Sternberg's work has made us anticipate the chronology of his films. We must double back to pick up the director on the day after his numerous set-backs, finally going under contract to Paramount, where he will make fourteen films, seven with Marlene Dietrich, and four with George Bancroft.

The legend, accredited notably by Jean Laserre in *La Vie brûlante de Marlene Dietrich,* has it that the meeting of the two men occurred fortuitously, when Bancroft, a lowly extra, was taking a shower, letting loose 'a formidable laugh, an inhuman laugh, enormous and savage, monstrous, a child's laugh and a murderer's laugh'.

Whatever the case, it seems that Bancroft appeared immediately to Sternberg as predestined for the role of Bull Weed, the gangster of *Underworld.*

Based on a story by Ben Hecht, *Underworld* is a film on the nocturnal nether regions of Chicago. Its hero is a brute with a thunderous laugh, as imposing and massive as his mistress is fragile and slight; she is nicknamed Feathers on acount of her taste in clothes.

Bull, who terrorises the elegant milieux of civilised banditry, is the friend of Rolls Royce, an alcoholic shyster lawyer. But the woman attempts to seduce the friend. In vain. What loyalty accomplishes, misunderstanding will betray: a feather in the lawyer's cigarette case.

Other men, however, also covet Feathers, notably the 'florist' Mulligan, front-man for the established gangs, threatened by Bull's tempestuous individualism. Mulligan, in the course of a gang ball, attempts to rape Feathers. Bull surprises him and kills him. But he is captured and sent to prison.

Having failed in an attempted escape engineered by his friends, Bull manages to go over the wall himself. Lying low at his friend's house, he believes himself betrayed by Feathers, going so far — since he understands the love that exists between them — as to sacrifice himself to protect their happiness. Barricaded in Rolls Royce's house, he puts up a heroic battle against the unleashed, better-armed forces of the police. When at last he is sure that the two lovers have been able to get away, Bull gives up. A cop taunts him: 'All that to gain one hour!' And the bandit replies simply: 'That one hour was worth more than all I've done in the rest of my life.'

With *Underworld,* Sternberg puts his thematic definitively in place: the sacrifice of one being for the one he loves but who loves another; the sacrifice of a mediator who builds the arch of alliance between two others from which he has been masochistically excluded.

In George Bancroft Sternberg finds the human symbol of rough purity, of the barbarous, telluric forces which permit the questioning of established orders. It is thus that Rolls Royce — another Sternbergian fantasy, but of refined elegance and of thoroughbred seductiveness — salutes Bull Weed in these terms: 'Attila the Hun at the gates of Rome'; giving the film added implications: 'You were born two thousand years too late.'

The depiction of hell is more valuable to Sternberg than the anecdotic aspect of a genre in the throes of formation. *Underworld* is less a first film about gangsters than a description of humanity at its different levels.

Moreover, less than a year after *Underworld,* Sternberg again takes up his two heroes Bancroft and Evelyn Brent for a film that is its apparent antithesis: *The Dragnet.*

The plot is symmetrical with that of *Underworld:* the woman, for love, betrays the gangster for the policeman. As for the latter, all his behaviour has ambiguous motives: the service of the law is for him no more than a pretext in his efforts to pull Maggie out of the mud of the Philadelphia underworld. But to do this he himself descends into the mire. The happy denouncement of the film is less a triumph for law and order than for love.

Comparison of *Underworld* and *The Dragnet* emphasizes the meanings that Sternberg intends to be given to his discourse. His films are not social denunciations, but an exploration of the motives of the heart.

Faced with the fragile but depraved and perverse Evelyn Brent, decked out in feathers, jewels, moire and satin, nestled in delicate furs, George Bancroft represents the sombre power of a formless virility, brandished like a blunt instrument.

That he has given a gangster and a policeman the same appearance proves that Sternberg does not section his moral universe into two primary certitudes. As Louis Chavance remarked in 1930: 'His detectives no more represent society than his gangsters constitute a symbol of revolt. There are two sides to a situation. It is the stronger who carry the day, and it would be stupid to choose between the double constraint of order and disorder.' (*La Revue du Cinéma,* No. 12.)

Moreover, in his next film, Sternberg raises George Bancroft from the shadows of hell, from the very bottom of the abysses. Does the stoker Bill Roberts not work below the waterline of the ship, in the soot, the slag, the flames and the coal of the boilers he feeds? . . .

The Docks of New York is one of those films by which the silent cinema testified that it had attained a sort of perfection: in Sternberg's work it occupies the privileged place of absolute masterpiece.

Inhabited by the internal rhythms of the images, constructed with rigorous precision where each detail reveals in the last instance its narrative necessity, where the most fortuitous incident is inscribed in the secret logic of the narrative, *The Docks of New York* illustrates the Sternbergian conception of cinematic *écriture* as a poem of lights and shadows, of dark waters and of chiaroscuro. The play of lighting on the sets and properties makes evident their multiple realities; the effects of light on faces reveals the tentativeness of a humanity never definitively acquired or given.

The plastic utilization of George Bancroft is, from this point of view, fully explicit, for the actor physically provides a statue of flesh, massive and granite-like, whose immutability is easily accepted. Begining with this block, Sternberg elaborates a personalist ethic that is the philosophical foundation of his work.

It is not FORCE, then, that interests Sternberg, as much as ENERGY, grasped in its dynamics. His conception of cinematic lighting is a vision of the movement of forms. There is what I called 'the internal rhythm of the images', just as one would have to talk of the internal rhythm of beings, as conceived over the course of their changes. Form, surface, and real volume do not change, but the displacement and the variation of zones of shade and light modify the meaning because they uncover the internal light of creatures and things.

In all the films that he made with Bancroft, Sternberg described his evolution as a birth of the person through the death of the character. In *Underworld,* death is almost physically expressed. In *The Dragnet* the character of the policeman 'dies' by resignation, then by degradation, before redemption. In *The Docks of New York* the strange love of one night is a death throe, a bearer of resurrection.

In speaking of Sternberg, I am deliberately using a vocabulary that is highly tinged with spirituality, because it is important to take note, with him, of a Judaic upbringing, capable of explaining his vision of the world, quite as much as the Judaism of Freud remains indissociable from his psychoanalytic discoveries.

Indeed, one reads in his memoirs that Sternberg as a child was given compulsory religious instruction, under the rod of a teacher whom he learned to fear more than Jehovah: 'We dared not open our mouths, with the result that the entire class developed loose bowels. Stalking the room with a ruler in his hand, sniffing at each pupil in turn, our persecutor would soon discover the culprit, and with a triumphant exclamation haul him out of his seat to escort him to a platform which never served any other purpose.' (*Fun in a Chinese Laundry,* p. 7.)

In the mind of the child are associated at the same time images of corporal punishment, embarrassing impressions of public exposure, sickeningly degrading situations (the smell of dung refers to the idea of death), and schooling itself: 'we learned to read and write Hebrew, a language five thousand years old, without knowing the meaning of a single word.' Thus is explained the initial proposal of looking for the essential factor lurking beneath the most common experiences.

With due regard for their differences, let us say that *The Docks of New York* is the equivalent for Bancroft of what *The Devil is a Woman* is for Marlene Dietrich: an extension to its very limit of an attitude of despair towards the inner nature of Woman and Man, both of them capable of feelings when they are brought in contact with one another, in certain circumstances which are themselves revealing.

Thus it is that in *Thunderbolt,* his first talking film, Sternberg used Bancroft again, giving him once more the role of a gangster who sacrifices himself for the sake of his loved one's happiness with another . . . Sternberg was constantly inquiring into the mystery of real strength, discovering in the end that, for man in general, in the highest meaning of life's adventure, physical force is nothing if it is not supported by the force of love; the latter is in itself capable of altering the course of life, while the former participates in transforming the world.

It is in this sense that Josef von Sternberg can and should be claimed by Surrealism. Moreover, taking as his own, perhaps unwittingly, the task of restoring those powers lost to Man by Woman, Sternberg progressively turns toward another side of the mystery of power. 'Often an incredible tension draws Sternberg's actress like a bow: love for the weakest, for the most debased, passion for one who hardly merits pity.' (Chavance, op. cit.)

Sternberg knows that the unfathomable marvel of Love resides in the willingness of certain beings to take upon themselves the rescue of the other: to plunge for his sake into the foulest, most loathsome mire, to return to the surface together and rediscover, as something suddenly pure and light, the air that till then they had breathed out of habit alone.

In a setting of mists and hanging nets, Bancroft plunges to the aid of Betty Compson who wants to die. At the end of the night, it is she who, in fact, will really have saved him, by the force of her love and by the fascination of her femininity. For, with Sternberg, the true force is in Woman, just as for Breton the New Eve will remake what Eve undid: 'There are cold and hard actresses who put a kind of unity into the work, those straight and haughty women who look upon life only from under lowered lashes. No event breaks through their indifference.'

At the time when Louis Chavance published these lines, Sternberg had just finished shooting *The Blue Angel* in Germany: they foretell of an encounter, fatal and decisive as all real encounters are of an impassioned and tragic creator with *la belle indifférente.*

STERNBERG — MARLENE

. . . The metamorphoses that the inconstancy and fickleness of Woman suggest are in reality only the desperate quest for the unique. Man desires that the loved woman be diverse and multiple for him; the nudity of the embrace will reaffirm her unity. He desires that the most feminine take on the troubling aspects of the androgyne. This is why Sternberg could contrive the 'masculine' appearances of Marlene in his films: in a dinner jacket in *Morocco,* dressed as a man in *Blonde Venus,* she even kisses

71

a woman spectator on the mouth; at the end of *The Scarlet Empress* she is a triumphant hussar.

Fundamentally this excessive sophistication is an attempt to express the subtlest essence. The polymorphism of appearances has as its effect in Sternberg's work the revelation of the truth and uniqueness of existence.

This is why *The Devil is a Woman*, both culmination and impasse, constitutes the sum of the relations between Sternberg and Marlene, while at the same time fixing limits which it would be fatal to transgress; it is the film where 'Love is disguised in the habit of Death'.

Freely adapted from the novel by Pierre Louys (*La Femme et le pantin*), this film again recounts a romantic triangle. During Carnival, Antonio, a wanted man, meets Concha Perez, a fatal beauty, unreal as well as fascinating. After having arranged a rendezvous with her, he discovers his old friend Pascal, sceptical and disillusioned, who reveals to him his own past as one of Concha's humiliated lovers. Of this former cigarette-roller, vulgar and shrill, e has made an artist whose charm captivates all men; and he has lost her. For her, he has abased himself, going so far as to break with his friends, as well as with his past.

Having decided to flee Concha, Antonio goes to the rendezvous to bid her adieu. Alas, charm works, and Antonio is lost. Pascal surprises his friend in the arms of his mistress and challenges him to a duel. Concha, who knows him to be a deadly shot, begs Pascal to spare Antonio. He does so, but Antonio fires, wounds Pascal, and is arrested. From the provincial governor, whom she charms and allures, Concha obtains the release of her friend, and two passports for France. At the border, however, Concha lets Antonio leave by himself, and returns to Pascal.

The melodramatic outline of the story should not conceal from us however the profound complexity of the relations woven among the three characters. A cruel ambiguity often links lovers, and the truth of the passions is often improbable. Linked forever to Pascal by her past, perhaps also by her remorse, certainly by gratitude in the conviction of having been made by him, Concha is one of Sternberg's most fascinating female characters. In any case, she is the one in which he has best analysed the myth of Pygmalion and Galatea. Pygmalion does not love Galatea, and the latter has with her creator only the contradictory relations of the child with the father. What Pygmalion does with Galatea is the mark of utter despair, since he tries to substitute appearance for reality, an idea of essence that he has made for himself. It is *for him* that Pygmalion desires Galatea, for she is the purifying concept of his fantasies. Thus, each man follows during a part of his life (sometimes the whole of his life) an imaginary femininity that will never be his. The idea of love that haunts Pygmalion is fundamentally onanistic, and Galatea is in the end no more than a mannequin for assuming the metamorphoses of the creator's fantasies. It is himself that Pygmalion pursues through the dream from which Galatea slips away.

The Devil is a Woman is the culmination of this order of approach. After this film, when Sternberg and Marlene decided (or had it decided for them by Paramount) not to work together any longer, Marlene became a myth and, as such, pursued on the screens a career quite independent of her life as a woman. Sternberg remained the capable director he had always been, with two strokes of genius still in him: *The Shanghai Gesture* and *The Saga of Anatahan* (*I, Claudius* would have been the third). Consequently it is as false to claim that Sternberg was finished after Marlene as to suggest perpetual and empty comebacks for Marlene after Sternberg.

But let's return to *The Devil is a Woman*. In Sternberg's mind the initial subject is a Caprice, that is, a composition in which inspiration and intuition are unbridled without any care for respecting the rules. The density of the sound-track, which consists of apparently chance recurrences of themes from Rimsky-Korsakov's 'Capriccio Espagnol' intertwined with folk-tunes and *paso-dobles toreros*, gives some idea of the work.

The sets, made of gratings, of hedges, cages, silhouettes of trees, misty dawns, rose-laurels and gloved hands, is suddenly broken by grotesque grimaces, hideous gnomes, or puppets animated as if better to accentuate the diaphanous beauty of Concha, but also better to externalise the emotional states of the masked lovers.

Spain, if it is not seen here except through clichés, commonplaces, and conventions, appears less as a setting than as a vision of the world, and more particularly, a vision of romantic relations: from 'La Celestina' (by Fernando de Rojas), Sternberg borrows a swarming microcosm of prostitutes, torero-pimps, and chivalrous hidalgos.

From Goya, he is inspired to produce a gallery of repugnant portraits, cruel etchings, or seductive but frivolous *majos* and *majas*, though he is aware in spite of it all that Goya, himself an author of 'Caprichos', described love as a universe of aggression, as a sabbath of horrors.

This contrapuntal reaching into the obscene and the foetid only emphasizes Sternberg's tireless course: through masks and contradictions to discover primary truth. 'A phenomenology of dissimulation', says Bachelard *(Le Droit de rêver, p. 202)*, 'must strike to the root of the will to be other than what one is.'

Concha Perez is the garden spider of this arachnidan universe. The whole film is a fabulous and immense spider's web, woven in full awareness by the director himself. The trees twist their crooked fingers, willows weep in languid foliage; contorted gratings enclose imprudent or uncaring lovers; mantillas ensnare with their lace, and in the shadow of a proliferation of streamers is the wakeful, venomous glance of the Spider Woman, desired as she is, and as she imprisons in the mortal toils of her web those who have dared the adventure, and whom she smothers.

Having reached the summit with *The Devil is a Woman*, Sternberg in his turn felt deprived of air. On April 14, 1935, *Pour Vous*, No. 333, published a statement by Marlene Dietrich which clarified the turning-point of the director's career: 'Mr. von Sternberg wants to make no more films for a while. He has a number of interests outside the cinema, especially painting. He wants to rest, and his opinion is that this is for me the best moment to begin to follow my own road.'. . .

STERNBERG THE OBSCURE

Upon having finished with Marlene Dietrich (and with his contract), Sternberg took the trouble and the time for a respite. Of short duration, it is true. He went from Paramount to Columbia, then undertook *I, Claudius* (which could have been a monument according to what we know and have seen of it), finally changing company for practically each of his later films.

With *Crime and Punishment,* Sternberg took on Dostoyevsky, but had to contend with the commercial exigencies of his employers.

Despite the interest that could have been aroused in him by this descent to the heart of metaphysical guilt, Sternberg could not make a personal work out of a ready-made script, a scenario he had had no hand in, and actors not of his choice. Possibly he was chosen because his knowledge of German facilitated his direction of the actors.

Besides, in this year, 1936, Hollywood was 'Germanising': numerous immigrants from Europe, especially Germans, were fleeing a regime that persecuted Jews and all those who still represented a certain ideal of liberty. Berlin definitively displaced Vienna as capital of the German world.

In the light of these apparently peripheral considerations, it is right to approach Sternberg's next film, the often deprecated *The King Steps Out,* a filmic adaptation of the famous Viennese operetta *Sissi.* There is no question that it is not a great film, but it is an interesting production in which, with complete freedom, Sternberg could use an assigned theme to abandon himself to personal nostalgia, to virtuosities of montage, even to several elaborate shots.

In the first scenes, flashing images show runaway horses dashing through the sunlight. At the ford of a river, a gallop throws up a shower of water, and we see a carriage tearing along through the countryside.

At court, a sumptuous palace recalls *The Scarlet Empress.* But the most carefully done part of the film is that which occurs in the little town in Bavaria where the archduke arrives for an incognito stay. Over the usual clichés of this *Mittel Europa* that seems to haunt Hollywood, Sternberg animates the operetta streets with joyful dresses, bestrews the parks and gardens with opulent floral displays, chisels the cast-iron gratings with sumptuous arabesques and prepares the peak of his film: a carnival touched by reminiscences of the Prater in Vienna.

In a setting of dancing balloons, a paper dragon passes by. Sissi and her archduke shoot and laugh, happily, while around them and within them the carnival reaches its zenith. Without seeming to do so, Sternberg remakes the scene from *Lena Smith*. Here is the haunted tunnel. The girl and the handsome officer rush to the hot sausage stand, wolf down pretzels. When overtaken by a patrol of singing soldiers, Sissi mingles with them. A lateral tracking shot that follows the group ends with Franz-Josef, who takes the girl into his arms and leads her into a waltz. The waltz is interrupted by a song in honour of the archduke's birthday, then begins again. They sit down out of breath in an arbour, when a gipsy arrives and foretells adventure for them.

This long sequence is dazzling, in rhythm and spirit; its virtuosity confirms the seriousness placed by Sternberg in even his minor productions or assignments. Finally, it illustrates the importance given to Festival in his dramaturgy.

There is practically no film by Sternberg where he has not fitted in a place for delirium or extravagant display; for him the function of Festival is inseparable from the imagination. Is not Festival the waking dream, something like a light in the night of living, something which illuminates a need for externalization of which in the final instance the work of art is also an aspect? Inseparable from the ethic of the mask, Festival is a moment of liberation of energy, an almost sacrificial moment, where man discovers a certain dimension of the sacred capable of clarifying his own search for self. The unconstrained freedom that it manifests, the galloping of an imagination without bitterness or remorse, makes of it a ritual of consumption in which obsession with the decay of the flesh is resolved. Because it purifies, Festival in Sternberg's work often precedes a bloody exorcism. Intoxication leads the desire for an other out to sea, away from the isles of ennui. Often, Festival parodies social ritual, shakes off the excessive bonds of convention. Sometimes it permeates the whole of a work.

Of Sternberg's uncompleted film one can scarcely speak. What remains (and is often seen on television) gives one to believe that a masterpiece was still-born. Of his intentions, Sternberg has explained at length in his memoirs, confirming the importance that he accorded the film, and clarifying his ethic: 'To show how a nobody can become a god, and become a nobody and nothing again, appealed to me.' (*Fun in a Chinese Laundry*, p. 173.)

Taking time to step back from his projects, Sternberg left himself open (as they say of a boxer who drops his guard). He will live to the end of his life haunted by the fear of letting it down again. He knew he had let it down.

After three years of silence, Sternberg agreed to parody himself once more with *Sergeant Madden*.

Basically, the scenario exploits the melodramatic complications of a cop's life. Much in the MGM style of the period, it belongs to the genre of the series of such productions as *Boys' Town*, and other children of the Hardy family by which the producers of good will supported New Deal politics in the elimination of the urban banditry consequent on the economic crisis, and with which the chiefs of MGM competed with the James Cagneys, Humphrey Bogarts, and other angels with dirty faces from the lawless streets of Warner Brothers. For all that, it is no less interesting to analyse, at the level of the script's intentions, the meanderings through which Sternberg unrolls his narrative. On the thematic level alone it is paradoxical to note that the commonest motives engender the most terrible fate: it is curious to see a film 'psychoanalysing' the process that makes a hooligan of the son of a policeman. Behind the shield of order, a criminal temperament entrenches itself. As for the heroine, whose name, Helena, recalls Lena Smith and Helen Faraday *(Blonde Venus)*, she lets us rediscover the constant theme of girls seduced and abandoned, as well as the theme of lost children, for whom Sternberg always showed an immense affection.

We must now leap ahead several years — to 1950 — to find the last film by 'Sternberg the Obscure', placing to one side for the moment the three exotic indicators of a tell-tale Far East: Shanghai, Macao, Anatahan.

Thus in 1950–1951, under contract to Howard Hughes, Sternberg made for RKO the indispensible anti-red film that every Hollywood director 'had' to do during the cold war: *Jet Pilot*, one more variation on what could have been an act of treason for love, comparable to *The Last Command* and, above all, to *Dishonored*. From successive alterations (five according to Ado Kyrou), *Jet Pilot* emerged drained of blood. Several sublime shots yet arise from the cadavre, yet one can no longer say what is Sternberg's. Certainly there is an aerial ballet where 'aircraft make love' (Kyrou), but we also know that Howard Hughes, enamoured of aviation, had many aircraft added to the final cut.

Finally, *Jet Pilot* was the only experiment in colour film in the work of Josef von Sternberg.

THE FAR AND THE EAST

Four films by Josef von Sternberg take place in the Far East. Three, in the fabulous setting of the international concessions, are alive with a strange fauna of soldiers of fortune, unscrupulous crooks, and high-class swindlers. For the setting of the last of them, the culmination of his work, Sternberg chose Anatahan:

> A lazy island where Nature bestows
> Peculiar trees and savoury fruit.[2]

76

In decadent civilisations, in the twilight of existence, on the doorstep of nothingness, the call of exoticism is the final solicitation of an earthly but mythical beyond. Before Sternberg others have heard of it, of whom Baudelaire was not the least.

From its beginning, Hollywood has devoted an important fraction of its production to Far Eastern exoticism; the Chinese have always played a role in it, sometimes disturbing, sometimes disconcerting, which without being crucial, participated in the disconcerting function of escapist cinema.

For his part, in 1932 Sternberg conjured up the Shanghai Express in the swarming, cosmopolitan streets of Peking. The rails sliced through shops with facades of daub, decorated with wicker traps, a slow but straightforward course, obstructed by the coolies' impassiveness.

The tumultuous China of the revolutionary years furnished him an exotic setting for the venomous, suggestive beauty of Marlene.

In 1941, that is with *The Shanghai Gesture*, he took one more step toward the opiatic mysteries of the Far East. This time, the action is situated in a luxurious gambling house, during the frenzied period of the Chinese New Year. Sternberg once again tells us the story of debasement: that of Poppy Smith, in reality the daughter of Sir Guy Charteris, a notable puritan who is fighting to close the Shanghai brothels. Among these is Mother Gin Sling's, the sophisticated house where the two worlds of the Orient and the Occident come together, the degraded and the profaner.

The vengeance of Gin Sling, proprietress of the place, is terrible; she has Poppy seduced by Omar, a professional rake, who uses gambling and alcohol to lead Poppy into corruption. On the occasion of an opulent banquet, which is to be a terrible and cruel revelation, Gin Sling has invited to her table all the occidental and oriental personalities of Shanghai, including Sir Guy. During dessert, the rear curtain rises on Poppy Smith, a veritable living sponge, sleepwalking human wreckage. Finally, Gin Sling wreaks her vengeance, but Destiny always knocks twice, for in a final *coup de théâtre*, Sir Guy reveals to Gin Sling that Poppy is in reality *their* own daughter. The nickname 'Mother' that her clients had given to Gin Sling suddenly acquires a fatal significance.

With *The Shanghai Gesture*, Sternberg raises the ambiguities of morality to a yet higher degree. The puritan inquisitor with a sordid spirit and the vile past of an adventurer without scruples; the proprietress of the house had been profaned as a girl when she had had pure, romantic dreams; the daughter sacrificed to debauchery and vice becomes the reeling symbol of degradation incarnating the hope of two young lovers rich in illusions.

In the house of chance, where the most refined are the most perverted, Sternberg has created a climate of disquieting appearances. Behind the hangings, around the tables, in the shadow of the smoking dens, at the feet of mysterious women with enigmatic pasts, in the frozen reflections of lacquers, beneath the shadowed ceilings from which hang shaded lamps, pass the inexpressible terrors of an irremediable involution.

There emanates from *The Shanghai Gesture* a narcissistic sense of intellectual onanism, as if through this film Sternberg had descended to the perdition of the self-satisfied mirror.

One gets a little of the same sense at the best moments of *Macao*. With a story that follows all the threads and all the ploys of adventure stories, Sternberg once more lingers in a port to listen to the foghorns of departing ships, to await the invitation to a voyage.

Like a lost albatross hoping for flight, on the wooden floats tossed about by a swell of filthy water, wanders Robert Mitchum, clad all in white. The immaculate rubs up against the revolting.

An old blind Chinese, in the cosmopolitan streets of the port, strokes with his dry fingers the rich flesh of Jane Russell of the mother of pearl skin. Horror dwells in the marble fascination of a pillar of flesh.

In the nightclub's motionless heat, tirelessly stroked by the ventilation fans like giant, slow propellors, sings an adventuress with a mane of hair, scented with sandal-wood, decked in jewels and spangled satin. One 'imagines the sweetness of going down there to live together'.

Sternberg's oriental films, as if in the heavy listing of junks at anchor, role and pitch in the grip of the temptation to flee, impatient to embark for the unknown.

The port beckons departure, but departure gets underway only for another port. The buckle closes by rediscovering the impasses of its own circle. Alone, out at sea, one island can still send out the almost posthumous appeal: Josef von Sternberg embarks in order to be quit of it.

Seven years after the end of the Pacific War, on the island of Anatahan, men still await the enemy who will never come. Around their absurd machine-gun the sergeant details a constant watch, which nothing any longer demands. But the enemy is there! One they do not suspect is there, with them. In them.

Because of a man and a woman on Anatahan, men will die, one after another, riven by hatred.

The discovery of a revolver in the wreckage of an airplane does not settle things: who possesses the weapon holds the others at his mercy.

In a universe of apocalyptic disintegration, the luxuriant, exotic vegetation seems to weave an enormous spider's web, where these poor creatures will be ensnared at the edge of madness.

It is reminiscent of the slow, solitary degradation of Luis Bunuel's *Robinson Crusoe*, at war with himself after having made his peace with nature.

And then one day, somewhere on the beach, the Woman disappears, until the boats and planes reappear to take each of them back home. Survivors of a Hiroshima of the passions.

78

The dredger, this time, brings up from the bottom of the Ocean of Wars the blinding truth of men, and lays it out to the incandescent sun, on the sands of boundless solitude. The 'Chart' of *Anatahan,* on which Sternberg himself designed the thematic structure of his film, definitively reveals the rigorous construction of his implacable message: twenty-two sequences under a *gaze* from above symbolized by the airplane, which is God. In a like manner, the *voice* of the artist is substituted for the Last Judgment, in order to comment on the behaviour of creatures left to shift for themselves, and to stand back from the game.

Throughout the film, the sky, the sea, the forest, and the mountain constantly form the precise limit of the absurd passions that dictate human behaviour, and of which Sternberg drew up the inventory:

'Military Discipline' (Sequence 9, November 1945: 'We had thrown off the yoke of discipline.')

'Desire' (Sequence 8: 'How would you like to be my bride tonight?')

'Jealousy' (Sequence 6: 'Who are you combing your hair for?')

'Nostalgia' (Sequence 7: 'Are you thinking of your home?' 'Yes, but not when I see you.')

'Surrender' (Sequence 10: 'Our country had faced the reality of defeat.')

'Violence' (Sequence 13: 'The day began with a harmless little ditty — a prelude to violence.')

On the 'Chart' each passion is marked by a more or less intense colour, the variations on intensity determining and conditioning the internal rhythm of the film. The woman alone is exempt from passions, but it is she who conditions or determines them all.

On the isle of Anatahan, Keiko (according to Claude Ollier) 'is the only clear-sighted, realistic, practical being.' (*Cahiers du Cinéma,* No. 168.) Appearing from the third sequence, she is *present* in all the ensuing scenes: when she does not figure in them physically, she lives in the motives of the men (save for the one Sternberg has condemned from the beginning: the sergeant who prefers the machine gun). From the discovery of the crashed airplane, Keiko will be the object of conquest, and legitimates every effort at possession.

Here we rediscover Sternberg's fundamental theme: salvation is modulated by the notion of wreckage. Henceforth he realises that salvation rests in detachment; solitude and scrutiny. Seven years on Anatahan, seven years of films with Marlene Dietrich, seven years from birth to the room in Hamburg, seven years is the exact duration of eternity; since it is the duration of the essence of things.

The sea, the forest, the sky, and the mountain are disincarnated under our eyes. The sea is already nothing but a sealed aquarium with myopic fish bumping into its sides.

The forest is only an inextricable intermeshing of fragile streamers, of captive strings, and of prisoner nets. The nothingness of the passions.

In the sky reigns the eye of Jehovah. Under this gaze of a superior indifference, human behaviour is only derisory and vain agitation.

The only certitude, perhaps, is the mountain. Its snowy summit, the only sign of purity. The final hope: the white page for which everything is possible. 'La chair est triste, hélas! et j'ai lu tous les livres.' The ocean breeze rises for the last appeal. 'Les oiseaux sont ivres d'être parmi l'écume inconnue et les cieux'; the nothingness of Mallarmean alabaster invites Sternberg to the arrogant silence of the disappointed gods. Already his heart no longer hears the song of the seamen belching out their surfeit of heavy beer on the dockside. The artist-Creator is weary.

Certain of the grandeur and the immensity of his work, disheartened by too much incomprehension, Sternberg throws into the face of the world his most perfect creation, perfect because disincarnated and abstract, and he offers to comprehending spirits the creative possibility of a fantasy henceforward without brake or rein. On the empty screen 'que sa blancheur défend' Sternberg finally decides that he will speak no longer. 'The ideal work of art is a blank screen on which each imagination in its turn can paint its own image.'

(translated by Peter Baxter)

Notes

1. Translator's note: except where otherwise indicated, quotations are from Josef von Sternberg, *Fun in a Chinese Laundry* (London; Secker and Warburg, 1965).
2. Charles Baudelaire, 'Parfum Exotique', in *Flowers of Evil*, trans. Geoffrey Wagner (Norfolk, Conn.: New Directions, 1946).

Morocco

(originally published in Cahiers du Cinéma, *No. 225 (November-December 1970), pp. 5–13)*

When we consider all this, we can well understand why at the moment Hollywood is the navel of the earth, being the only place where people think of nothing else but amusing the rest of the world, turning out those sow's ears we take for silk purses . . . Hollywood is also the last boudoir where philosophy, become masochistic, can still find that laceration to which, fundamentally, it aspires: as by virtue of an unavoidable illusion it seems impossible, in fact, to discover anywhere else in the world women so unnatural, gross, impossible. The fact is that daily the whole world casts money at their feet so that they won't desert us, just as once it did at the feet of statues of gods or saints. A melancholy way of trusting the heart's salvation to a mirage of tinsel.

Georges Bataille

I METHOD

1. The present article continues our work on the re-reading of the classic Hollywood cinema which was initiated by our text on John Ford's *Young Mr Lincoln* (No. 223). We saw John Ford's film as exemplary in that it showed an ideological enounced *(énoncé)*[1] subverted by the stress effects of the Fordian writing *(écriture)*. *Young Mr Lincoln* represented the ethical-political face of the capitalist and theological field of Hollywood cinema. *Morocco* on the other hand represents its erotic face, as a film that takes its place within the Sternberg oeuvre — an oeuvre produced by Hollywood, for forty years the major site of production of the erotic (fetishist) myths of bourgeois society and as such, itself fetishised and mythologised.

In other words, our reading of *Morocco* will distinguish the effects — inscribed with exceptional clarity here, even for Hollywood — implied by its kinship (the modes of which will be examined) with the bourgeois (but equally feudal) fictions produced by Judeo-Christian civilisation, founded on the Law of the Father, and characterised particularly by the role assigned to the woman.

On this point we will cite what Julia Kristeva has written on the historical transition (in the 14th century) from the epic enounced to that

81

of the novelesque; in other words, the transition from a civilisation of the symbol to a civilisation of the sign (in *Semiotica*, I, IV, 1969: 'Narration et Transformation'). The novelesque model and the system of the sign she describes have, despite the deconstruction to which they have been subjected, continued to be dominant and were especially so in Hollywood in 1930. Kristeva defines the transition in question as marked by the 'justification of one only of the terms of opposition: the Other (the Woman), into which the One[2] (the Author, the Man) projects himself and with which he fuses. An exclusion of the Other is immediately produced which inevitably presents itself as an exclusion of the woman, a non-recognition of sexual and social opposition.' Within this system, Woman is a 'pseudo-centre, a mystificatory centre, a blind spot whose value is invested into the One, who gives himself the Other (the centre) in order to live as one, single and unique. From this flows the exclusively positive quality of the blind centre (the Woman) which reaches the infinite (in nobility, and qualities of the heart), effacing disjunction (sexual difference) and dissolving into a series of *images* (from angel to Virgin). . . . the idealisation of the Woman (the Other) signifies a society's refusal to shape itself by acknowledging the *differential* but *non-hierarchical status* of the opposed groups, and equally, that society's structural need to give itself a permutative centre, an *other* entity whose only value is that of *object of exchange* among equals. . . . This devaluing valorisation prepares the ground for, and does not basically distinguish itself from, the explicit devaluation of which woman was the object from the 14th century onwards in bourgeois literature (in mediaeval verse tales, satires and farces).' As we know, such devaluation is reasserted quite particularly in Hollywood mythology (e.g. the ingenue, the vamp, the femme fatale). Here the 'pseudo-centre' Kristeva speaks of is the *fetish,* and our text will attempt to distinguish all its occurrences in Sternberg's film (cf. IV.2). This reciprocal absorption of the One and the Other (the Author and the Woman) within an effacement of sexual difference accounts for (and implies) the fact that the Masquerade, Virile Display and Inversion[3] are the erotic paradigms of *Morocco* (cf. Lacan, 'La signification du phallus': 'Paradoxical as this formulation may seem, I am saying that it is in order to be the phallus, that is to say, the signifier of the desire of the Other, that a woman will reject an essential part of femininity, namely all her attributes in the masquerade'; and 'The fact that femininity finds its refuge in this mask by virtue of the fact of the repression *(Verdrängung)* inherent in the phallic mark of desire, has the curious consequence of making virile display in the human being itself seem feminine').

2. In *Young Mr Lincoln* the diegetic process (the progressive setting in place of a device functioning as a snare, the substitution of one mode of narration for another in the course of the fiction, the narrative *coups de* *force* involving a decisive role for the diachronic dimension) called for a reading in terms of its chronological development, since the fictional structures in it were transformed by the narration. In *Morocco*, inversely, as we shall see, the structures of the fiction (cf. section II) are programmed from the outset and are simply repeated with variations in their successive realisations. This justifies us in considering *Morocco* as a text which can be read synchronically, since the key determinations of the fiction can all legitimately be brought together at once within a complete set of their realisations.

II STRUCTURE OF THE FICTION

1. To elaborate the structures of a fiction like *Morocco*, we cannot but base ourselves on what constitutes its major enounced: the fictional 'novelesque' situations considered within their double — erotic and social — determination (the La Bessière — Amy Jolly — Brown triangle, and the secondary triangle, Caesar — Mme Caesar — Brown). And in fact, the erotic relations occur within the framework of a rigorously delineated social situation which is not a neutral backdrop, but which, on the contrary, *determines these erotic relations and is in turn determined by them*. In other words: the double erotic/social determination of the fictional situations and the *double inscription* of the discourse of *Morocco*, are such that their reciprocal determining relations are articulated according to a *logic* (impossible to abstract from the text without relapsing into mechanistic structuralism) which is internal to the scriptural process, and distinguishable in the recurring effects of meaning produced by this double inscription.

2. The *social determinations* of the different characters and the relations these generate between them are organised according to a strict hierarchy which we will describe here while clearly accepting (see II, 1) that this hierarchy is going to be perverted by the erotic determinations. From top to bottom of the social scale within the fiction we have: a) the European upper middle class (La Bessière: rich enough to 'buy up all Morocco', 'citizen of the world', dilettante painter — 'He would be a good painter if he were not so rich'); b) the colonial upper middle class (the group of La Bessière's friends who, at the cabaret, are shocked by the 'democratic tastes' of La Bessière, who leaves them to go and sit at Caesar's table; guests at the dinner party to celebrate the engagement, including a general in the French Army); c) the native bourgeoisie; d) officers of the Legion (Captain Caesar); e) the owner of the cabaret, who occupies an intermediary position between the two categories (see IV); f) the lower strata, i.e. the (miserably paid) legionnaires, the Moroccan crowds, the dancers-singers-prostitutes of the cabaret, and the women of the Legion's 'rearguard'.

It should be noted that while the masculine characters of the fiction have a fixed social status (not modified by the erotic determinations), the social position of the women is fluid: Mme Caesar seems to have been through the experience of a drop on the social ladder before her marriage replaced her within category d); Amy Jolly, herself fallen — from a relatively elevated rank (at least in terms of wealth, e.g. reference to her mink coat) — to category f), is again to be promoted to the highest position by the circumstance of her coming marriage to La Bessière, and again drops to the lowest to become one of the 'women without hope' who follow the soldiers.

3. As for the *erotic determinations*, these set up two homologous triangles: La Bessière — Amy Jolly — Brown; Caesar — Mme Caesar — Brown. The erotic situations inscribed in these two triangles are in their turn over-determined socially; in other words, the set of relations to which the situations of these characters give rise are inscribed into the pattern of *Morocco* and at the same time produce it (the reciprocal interaction indicated above).

It is possible to see a series of homologous relationships:

La Bessière, diffident lover of Amy Jolly/Caesar, the deceived husband;
Amy Jolly/Mme Caesar, both equally declassé by their deviant erotic behaviour which assimilates them with the prostitutes;
Amy Jolly, in love with Brown although courted by La Bessière and then engaged to him/Mme Caesar, also in love with Brown, i.e. with a man hierarchically inferior to her husband.

In other words, in all cases the object of desire is of inferior status to the desiring subject:

La Bessière, in love with a fallen women, has perhaps also been the lover of Mme Caesar;
Caesar is deceived by a wife for whom there is every ground for supposing that before her marriage she was in the same situation as Amy Jolly;
Amy Jolly and Mme Caesar both pursue a declassé, i.e. Brown.

The inscription of these hierarchical erotic relations brings into play:
1) Europeans with social status/declassé Europeans:

La Bessière — Mme Caesar
La Bessière — Amy Jolly
Caesar — Mme Caesar
Mme Caesar — Brown

Amy Jolly — Brown

(Although, like Brown, they belong to the category of the declassés, Mme Caesar and Amy Jolly have, have had, or could have, access to a higher social rank — a possibility from which Brown seems to be excluded, which 'downgrades' him in relation to them.)

2) Europeans/Moroccans:

Legionnaires — Moroccan women

We will simply note a point here, in order to return to it later (cf. IV, 1) — the interaction between 1) and 2). For example the ambiguity of Mme Caesar's racial type and dress, the character she plays in a sense representing a compromise between the Europeanness incarnated by Amy Jolly (Aryan) and the 'orientalness" (Morocco = Other than the West) incarnated in the fiction by the Moroccans whose dress she adopts.

4. Moreover, the play of the double, erotic-social, web is not produced independently of its *topographical* inscription. This inscription is effected along two axes: one vertical, and — within the Town — linking (by establishing a hierarchy) the High (La Bessière's palace) to the Low (the cabaret), while the cabaret itself is divided into a 'high' and a 'low' (the pit); the other, horizontal (Town/Desert).

5. a) The movement of desire works from high to low: towards the lower strata (cabaret, prostitutes); b) access to the desert implies a passage through the lower strata: in particular, Amy Jolly only gets there after having first found and then re-found Brown, in the cabaret and then in a seedy café; c) it is therefore *in the depths* that desiring subjects discover the *object* of their desire; and in the fiction, the desert is inscribed as the pure signifier of that desire — that is, as a mirage, a snare, always evoked but never shown until the final scene. Thus in Amy Jolly's room when Brown wishes to provoke her desire he literally 'lures' her with an evocation of the desert (he goes to the window and says 'you can smell the desert this evening' and then runs his fingers through his hair). The inscription of the Legion and Brown as 'vanishing' (see IV, 2) is a correlative of the desert's function as a snare: cf. the remark by La Bessière about the women camp followers: 'And very often when they do (catch up with them) they find their men dead.'

6. The fictional matrix we have just established (i.e. social/erotic/ topographical determinations) is not specific to this film, nor to Sternberg — even though some of the modes of its inscription are specific (cf. IV). It emerges as the variation and transformation of a structure whose other occurrences could be distinguished equally well in a) popular novels of the beginning of the century (indeed even in *La Recherche du temps perdu*), b) in numerous films produced between the beginning of the cinema and the thirties (Feuillade, Murnau, Lang, etc.). The transformation lies mainly in the fact that the fictional axis (High/Low — Desirer/Desired) is here reduplicated (High/Low + Town/Desert); the relation Town/Desert emerges as an ideological re-marking of the structure (ideological in the sense that the structuring function of the twofold erotic/sociological determination is almost masked by the fact that the over-inscription of the horizontal Town/ Desert axis is reduced to a purely erotic phantasy — i.e. the return to Nature as the locus of desire, as opposed to the town). It ought to be borne in mind that *Morocco* was produced, seen, and continues to be seen, solely as a love film (cf. its French title: *Coeurs brûlés*) and moreover that it to some extent borrows its fictional elements from the melodrama genre.

As far as the effects of this transformation are concerned, they emerge within a process of inscription which operates with the aid of constantly reduplicated batteries of signifiers:

Europeans — Moroccans (cf. 2);
Old World — New World: Brown typed as an American, in opposition to La Bessière and Caesar who are men of Old Europe;
Characters with social status/declassé or displaced characters;
Even at the visual level: grids and screens (towns)/uniform white expanse (desert).

These effects consist in reduplicated journeys (cabaret — desert; desert — cabaret), in a proliferation of rhymes and inversions (which are implicated in the structural relations here, and are not just a decorative surplus as in the case of other Sternberg films). They also consist in characters who produce a *mediation* between the two axes and the multiple sets of signifiers which overdetermine them. This does not necessarily mean that these characters have the function of 'intermediaries' *in the fiction* (as is the case for La Bessière and the owner of the cabaret, cf. IV, 1), but that they ensure within the logic of the text a mixing of erotic and/or racial determinations (for example, Mme Caesar, cf. 3; the owner of the cabaret 'Lo Tinto', cf. IV, 1).

III MYTHOLOGICAL DETERMINATIONS

1. In the forefront of the mythological determinations is the historical role of the star in the Hollywood system and its articulation within the Sternbergian fiction. It can be said of any star that the process of fetishistic eroticisation which defines them as such assigns them a relatively restricted number of possible types of fiction in which their presence then has the function of *operator*[4]: the fictional elements of the star-film are to a large extent the re-investment of what a star's preceding films and, equally, extrafilmic life, have inscribed as a *role* credited to the particular actor or actress. But instead of confirming the specialisation implied by such repetition, the inscription on the contrary seeks to mask it and to present it as difference, indeed as a 'first time'; from one film to the next, the presence of the star transcends the filmic/extra-filmic opposition, but the films themselves emerge as a constant denial of that transcendence, while at the same time making use of the recognition effects it implies: here, for instance, as in her preceding film *The Blue Angel*, and in her extra-filmic life, Marlene is a cabaret singer.

a) The effects of recognition are therefore produced by her status as cabaret singer with reference to *The Blue Angel*, as well as by the inscription within the fiction of the transformation wrought upon her by Sternberg (multiple allusions to her recent worldly past). The heroine thus enjoys a capital of past history (wealth, erotic success) which she is progressively to squander — the production of these effects of recognition being directly overdetermined by the mythology and the themes set in motion by Sternberg, which are precisely those of 'fall' and squandering.

b) In fictional terms, the operation of denial is inscribed by setting in motion a double principle of variation:

The scene where Marlene appears produces a *narrative and iconographical* break in the sense that: 1) the preceding scene (the Legion's arrival in town, Tom Brown arranging a meeting with a Spanish woman), is interrupted just at the point of follow-up (shot of the raised hands of a dancer holding castanets which is left unexplained); 2) it is succeeded by an empty shot of the port (noise of a siren) which functions like a placard announcing the not very readable scene that follows; 3) iconographically, this scene is produced in paradigmatic opposition to the entire beginning of the film: sun/night, dry/damp, land/sea, dust/smoke; i.e. South/North; 4) it is to be read as flowing from a previous fiction (the arrival of Marlene in Morocco is explicitly presented as the substitute for a suicide, the dénouement of the absent fiction).

While Marlene is, as in *The Blue Angel*, a cabaret singer, the singer status is here socially and erotically overdetermined in an inverse sense to *The Blue Angel*: the cabaret-suicide association implies a defeat which puts Amy Jolly in closer analogy with Professor Unrat than with Lola Lola, and this clearly is bound to have some connection with the Amy Jolly-Brown erotic relation.

This double process of recognition-denial confers on the star a fictional place which is obviously determining for the dramatic level, but one that is played out less as an *activity* than as its *deferment*.

In other words, by her inscription within the fiction, her incarnation as protagonist, her placement in relation with other characters, the star

87

compromises her identity-in-itself (i.e. her being-as-star) and puts into play her 'value'. The inscription therefore consists in a *deferment* of her signification (her 'value') as star within the production of a *surplus* (her becoming-*actress* and *protagonist*); a surplus which is however transferred back to her credit insofar as the fictional effects produced (by her gestures, the course she traces in the film, her relations with the other characters) are in the last analysis constrained to signify her as 'star'. This is marked by the *austerity of the star's acting* (parsimony of gesture, restricted number of partners, a closing-off — particularly accentuated in Sternberg — of the fictional place, which serves like a display-case); in other words few fictional effects are produced which are not required to valorise her.

Sternberg's films occupy a particular place within the star system because it was Sternberg himself who produced Marlene as star, contrary to the majority of Hollywood film makers (including some of the greatest) who ultimately did no more than ensure the circulation of the value we have just discussed. What does Sternberg himself say about this? 'Don't tell me that Marlene fills my work, that she runs away with it, that she possesses it and drives it . . . Marlene is not Marlene in my films, let's get that clear. Marlene is not Marlene, Marlene is me, and she knows that better than anyone.' (*Cahiers*, no. 168.) Such assertions, which seem to denigrate the star system, in fact do no more than reflect its ideology, while at the same time perverting it, inasmuch as the author Sternberg appropriates to himself the value of the star, which he can thenceforward only consider as the devalued surplus of his work. So that if he speaks of her as fetish, it can only be in the mode of a violent denial.

This phantasy representation by Sternberg of his relations with Marlene is inscribed in all the key moments of the fiction of *Morocco*, on the one hand in the character of La Bessière, who is, first of all physically, Sternberg's double. From the start (scene of the arrival of the boat), La Bessière sets himself up as the protector and suitor of Marlene (he gives her his card — i.e. his name). Thereafter, La Bessière is insistently presented as a man who does not want to be taken over by a woman (he has the reputation of being a hardened bachelor); he does nothing to restrain Amy Jolly and even drives her to Brown in his car. In other words, he himself pushes to its limits the process of devaluation of Amy Jolly which was marked from the beginning of the film. On the other hand these same phantasies of devaluation are inscribed in the relation between Amy Jolly and Brown, who first assimilates her with the prostitutes he habitually frequents ('I always pay for what I get'), and considers her on their model as his thing — an assimilation which the end of the film renders effective. And this can be related to the following statement by Sternberg: 'When I finished *The Blue Angel* I had finished with Marlene. I didn't want to make another film with her. But she followed me back onto home territory as most women do, and I had to direct her in *Morocco*.'

2. Another type of Sternberg phantasy has to be taken into account, which constitutes a masochistic variant on the one just described: the phantasy of abandonment (La Bessière is abandoned by Amy Jolly in the same way that Caesar is deceived by his wife). Both phantasies have a structuring function in the fiction inasmuch as they directly determine the erotic situations, but also inscribe themselves in the breaks in the fiction in an unpredictable and emphatic way:

> when Caesar, having vainly attempted to make Brown confess, himself utters his wife's name in front of all the protagonists;
> in the same way, in front of his guests, La Bessière confesses his absolute submission to the caprices of Amy Jolly ('You see . . . I love her; I'd do anything to make her happy.')

These two scenes, in their term for term correspondence to each other, produce a double transgressive effect: — a transgression of the social codes through public admission of distress, of defeat, of irremediable loss, above all when this is located in the erotic order; and equally, transgression of the Hollywood fictional codes to the extent that these, to meet the dramatic requirements, re-assert those social codes (telling a story means postponing the confession, solution, cause, etc.).

Insofar as these phantasies systematically devalue the object of desire *and* pose that object as unattainable, they are able to have a structuring action in a fictional field where a hierarchy of relations is inscribed that goes as far as their total disjunction.

IV INSCRIPTION[5]

1. The inscription of the signifiers of Westernness and Easternness. (This diagram only takes into account the 'characters' implicated in the over-determined social-erotic relations outlined in II, 3.)

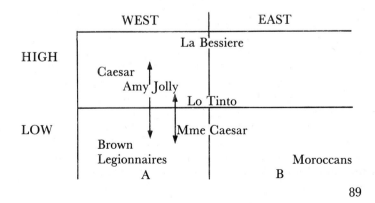

In their physical typing, Amy Jolly and Caesar represent the old world of (northern) Europe (they are 'Aryans');

Brown (the name, gestural typing) represents the New World;

Easternness is only represented by the Moroccan women (dancers, singers, prostitutes, the 'rearguard');

Although the Moroccans feature episodically in the fiction (crowds at prayer, rich bourgeoisie, Mme Caesar's hired men beaten up by Brown), they do not enter into the erotic relations which constitute the fictional web;

La Bessière, presented as French, is placed in A for the same reason as Amy Jolly and Caesar; however, physically he is a Latin (Amy Jolly and Caesar are Nordic). Moreover, as a Frenchman *he has a relationship with Morocco* (Amy Jolly and Caesar have run aground there and remain alien to it except, in the case of Amy Jolly, for the last shot). He has a *knowledge* of Morocco (implied in his status as one of the master class, the correlative of a blindness — his knowledge is exclusively concerned with the 'horizontal axis', cf. II, 6 — he knows what the 'rearguard' is, but is ignorant of the 'crimes of the lower orders');

Finally, two characters who are intermediary between A and B: Mme Caesar (cf. II, 4), and the owner of the cabaret, Lo Tinto — a Levantine, strongly typed in dress and physique (ridiculous evening dress, ring in his ear).

a) It is worth recalling that on the level of social determinations, the three characters who represent the Old World have, or have had, an elevated social position. While Brown, who represents the New World, occupies the lowest position on the scale of representatives of Westernness (without there ever being any allusion made to his drop on the social scale).

On the other hand, the Moroccans occupy the lowest position on the scale of representatives of Easternness.

b) On the level of erotic determinations, in conformity with a Western mythological tradition, an exclusively feminine value is assigned to the East.

The relationship of femininity to virility undergoes an inversion with reference to the phallocentric phantasy of bourgeois society (an inversion whose relative frequency in bourgeois *fictions* is moreover notable) by virtue of the fact that Brown (cf. a)) occupies a very much inferior social position and is the object of desire of Amy Jolly;

note that Lo Tinto's mixed race, like La Bessière's morphotype, are correlatives of their signs of inversion (the preciosity of La Bessière's behaviour and gestures, Lo Tinto's portly physique and his mother-cum-brothel-keeper behaviour vis à vis Amy Jolly);

their inscription into the fictional situation makes the three characters representing the Old World into signifiers of castration: La Bessière and

Caesar inasmuch as they lose their women, Marlene as fetish (note 2, below; that the impossibility of a return to Europe for Brown is linked to the fact that civil dress *would signify* his castration);

the dynamics of the fiction put the women into circulation from West to East and from the Old World to the New: it is the American who has all the women, who themselves rejoin the Orient as their mythic locus.

2. As we have seen (cf. 1) the critique of the fetishism of value, in an 'artistic' discourse produced within the capitalist system (and indeed in a location — Hollywood — where fetishism is subject to a displacement, from commodity onto characters, which generalises the circulation of exchange value onto bodies and individuals), is carried out only in the mode of an erotic fiction itself entirely determined by the ideology. But the — of course intra-ideological — critical effect is readable today only because it was *wrought* within a fiction which is simultaneously erotic *and social*. (Whereas a solely erotic determination would never have been able to produce anything except an effect of specular duplication.)

a) All values in *Morocco* are fetishes: money, jewels, clothes, woman (star). However, it is not just the Sternbergian inscription which produces them as fetishes; they flow directly from fields (social, cultural, psychological — external and anterior to the film) in which they are already constituted as fetishes. Moreover, the reactivation of their fetishist nature by the Sternbergian fiction does not exhaust their value within that inscription — rather it preserves and accentuates it. The Sternbergian fetish, therefore, does not inscribe itself into the fiction *solely* as a signifier of castration[6] — it is not solely involved in the trajectories of the erotic (as their cause). Note inversely, how in Lang the inscription is strictly localised at the intersection of all the erotic and topographical trajectories (cf. the diamond in *Moonfleet*, the android of *Metropolis*, etc.).

It follows therefore that in Sternberg, and in *Morocco*, the fetish object or character is not inscribed according to a social/erotic topography as rigorous as that of Lang, even though it is always in the locations of desire (the cabaret and the desert, cf. II, 4) that the fetish functions as the cause of that desire; this is because it also gives rise to inscription effects which are not implied by the narrative logic. (In later films, like *Blonde Venus* or *The Devil is a Woman*, these effects, now purely plastic, managed through a proliferation of veils, feathers, baubles, etc., to parasitise the narrative itself, and in extreme cases, to devour it.)

For example, it will be noted how Amy Jolly denies the jewels offered her by La Bessière their erotic value, so that from there on they denote only Amy Jolly's accession to the bourgeoisie.

b) Thus in *Morocco*, the fetishes literally function simultaneously as *both* bourgeois value *and* erotic signifiers; they are therefore inscribed both as inalienable values, not capable of being squandered, *and* as signifiers of that squandering.

In Sternberg's films and therefore in *Morocco*, the fetish nature (of the object and the character) is exclusively concerned with what relates to Marlene, her body, her clothes, her make-up, her sophistication, her adornment. For *Morocco* in particular, note:

1) that the power of seduction and fascination that Marlene exerts (first cabaret scene, where she is literally presented as elusive and untouchable by anyone other than Brown), and the fetishisation which it entails are in proportion to her *inaccessibility*. Freud in his 'On Narcissism'[7] has described 'such women' who 'have the greatest fascination for men, not only for aesthetic reasons, since as a rule they are the most beautiful, but because of certain interesting psychological constellations'. This (inseparable) seduction and refusal are the correlatives of the constitution of a *system of signs*, of *marks* which are closed, artificial, coherent and self-sufficient;

2) note too that this system of signs has to be broken down (i.e. it has to lose its closed nature, its perfection) for the desire aroused by Marlene to cease to come within the order of fetishism and this time to inscribe her into the metonymic *signifying chain* of desire. Quite clearly, for the reasons cited at the beginning of this paragraph, this 'criticism' of fetishism can only be carried out in the last analysis — and this in spite of all mirages, masks, etc. — from a standpoint which is itself fetishist, which does not absolve us from having to describe its mechanism.

Each time therefore that Sternberg wishes to show us Amy Jolly in a non-fetishist erotic situation (the non-fetishism is illusory, as we have just seen), she begins to be 'squandered'; she offers Brown an apple, she gives him her key, she breaks her pearl necklace, she throws off her shoes. The fetishist nature of this 'critique' of fetishism is marked in the fact that Amy Jolly's rejection of her accessories immediately makes them rise retroactively to become fetish-objects in their turn. What results from all this? The impossibility for Sternberg to inscribe into his fiction the idealist statement which seems to be implied by his 'critique of fetishism' (i.e. return to nature, renunciation on the part of the woman of her accessories, her middle class social status — all that was in the air in the heyday of attempts to capture Sternberg for surrealism, cf. Ado Kyrou). An impossibility which rises from the fact that the moralising inscription of the renunciation of her accessories (necklace, shoes) is overdetermined by the inevitable inscription of these same accessories as fetish-objects which renew the chain of desire.

It must be noted here that this closed economy in which the formal fetishism and the anti-fetishist ideology constantly refer back to each other is translated by a fetishisation of the film locus (conceived as a precious 'little box', a jewel case, etc.) and plastic effects (play of light, masks, veils, etc.) which in the last analysis constitute *the image itself* as mask, gauze, screen — a total effect in which one can distinguish everything that has determined the fetishist appeal of Sternberg's films and to which, either in order to reject it as a 'fancywork' aesthetic, or to valorise it as style, critics have reduced the Sternbergian writing.

The vicious circle of a reciprocal critique of the ideology of 'natural purity' by fetishism and of fetishism by that ideology, thus emerges as strictly interminable within the framework of the bourgeois capitalist system into which Sternberg fits. (From which one can see how great a misunderstanding prevented Hollywood from recognising Sternberg as one of its own, the myth of the *artiste maudit;* accrediting him with a fringe position which is no more than a false front). It is this very impasse which nourishes the fiction of *Morocco,* and most especially, the relations of Amy Jolly and Brown which can only be resolved in a flight-pursuit between the two characters: one (Amy Jolly) never able to produce herself except as fetish, the other (Brown) never able to produce himself other than as mirage. (The elusive nature of the latter is underscored by two written inscriptions — the first 'I changed my mind', trace of his disappearance; the second, Amy Jolly's name engraved on the table in the café, both a trace of his passing through and a signal for the resumption of her pursuit which is by definition endless); as an ideological figure, he has no place in the fetishist field of Amy Jolly, and can only signify by his absence or his flight the impossible elsewhere — the Desert of pleasure [*jouissance*] and of death — where the fetishism of the woman would no longer be valid currency. Hence no doubt the accent this film brings to bear on the demand for love; that is, on an erotic relationship without a price, but for which Dr Lacan has taught us that the love offered is nothing other than the gift of what one does not have.

(translated by Diana Matias)

Notes

1. This use of the term *énoncé* derives from a distinction made by the French linguist Emile Benveniste, between *énonciation* ('enunciation') and *énoncé*. *Enonciation* is the act whereby an utterance is produced, and *énoncé* means what is thereby uttered in itself. (trans.)

2. Although for want of an adequate English term this has been rendered as 'the One', Kristeva's opposition is not between *l'Un et l'Autre* but between *le Même et l'Autre*, because she is applying her concepts to the text rather than to the individual. For an amplification of her use of this term see Kristeva's *Le Texte du roman* (The Hague; Mouton, 1970), p. 60. (trans.)

3. On the notion of masquerade we refer to Joan Riviere, 'La féminité en tant que mascarade' (*La Psychanalyse,* no. 7) [translated as 'Womanliness as a masquerade' in *Psychoanalysis and Female Sexuality,* edited with an introduction by Dr Hendrik M. Ruitenbeek (Newhaven, Conn.; College and University Press Services, 1966)] and to Michèle Montrelay, 'Recherches sur la féminité' (*Critique,* no. 278): 'Within this piling up of dotty objects, feathers, hats, strange baroque constructions which rise like so many silent insignia, a dimension of femininity takes shape which Lacan, taking up Joan Riviere's term, designates as *masquerade.* But it must be seen that the end of such a masquerade is to say nothing. Absolutely *nothing.* And in order to produce this nothing a woman uses her own body to disguise herself.'

4. The authors are here using 'operator' in its mathematical sense, defined as 'a symbol indicating an operation'; an 'operation' in mathematics being the subjection of a number to a process affecting its value, e.g. multiplication. (trans.)

5. In French, *l'écriture*– literally 'writing', but this is too general to give the sense of the process whereby meaning is inscribed into the text. (trans.)

6. See Freud's text 'Fetishism', *Standard Edition of the Complete Psychological Works of Sigmund Freud* (London; Hogarth Press, 1953–73), Vol. 21, and Lacan, 'La Signification du phallus', in *Ecrits* (Paris; Seuil, 1966).

7. Freud, *Standard Edition*, Vol. 14.

LOUIS AUDIBERT

The Flash
of the Look

(originally published in Cinématographe, *No. 25 (March 1977), pp. 7–12)*

A SINGULAR PRIVILEGE

There is a paradox concerning the close-up in classic film theory. It is one that is true of pure theoreticians whether or not they themselves are filmmakers (Eisenstein, Epstein, Eichenbaum, Balazs), and also of historians who explicitly or not have always been motivated by a certain normative intention (Bazin, Mitry). Indeed all these names can be cited, despite differences or real divergences, as indices of a common project constituted by a double movement: — a fixation toward the origin, or origins, that speaks of a search for the initial moment (even if it is sometimes multiple) of the crystallization or conquest of the cinema's *essence* in a decisive and absolute passage from a technological prehistory; — similarly, this essence has always been seen as that of a language, inevitably leading to the supposition of a *language-system,* defined either very strictly (cf. among others the cine-stylistic of Tynyanov and Eichenbaum), or as an ensemble of codes delimiting a certain number of possible figures.

Within this project, mention of the close-up is precisely that of a privileged figure which in an exemplary way accomplishes the *leap*, the passage, giving access to the essence and the truth of the cinema. Because of it, and thanks to it, the semantic capacity of filmic discourse is organised. Tynyanov writes, 'Close-ups are, so to speak, the subject and the predicate of the cine-sentence.' Eisenstein recalls and emphasizes the artistic change brought about by Griffith in making the first narrative insertions of the close-up. On this point, Jean Mitry, after so many others, will only follow Eisenstein.

Nevertheless, classic theory — this is one of its characteristic points — has then been led to curtail, reduce, repress this privilege of a unit, however important it has been to the advent of the cinema. This repression works in several ways: the historian who empirically notes its relative scarcity — a paradox — naturally concludes the impossibility, even the absurdity, of a continuous series of close-ups, or of the frequent

95

repetition of such a shot. He likes to see in it only a submission to the star-system — the vanity of the star — or he searches for its basis in a theory of the homogenisation of space. We know that, on this point, Mitry accords with Bazin in condemning and prohibiting a shot series in which the close-up would not be justified by a preceding shot in the series. And though his position may generally be more complex, Eisenstein expresses the same attitude in emphasising the necessity of bringing together different points of view in order to re-structure the unity of the represented space.

In all this, then, there is a wide-spread and paradoxical resistance. How to interpret it? In confronting this problem, it has been remarked up till the present that the close-up always functions as an extreme fragmentation of the scene, as a dispersal of what is represented, and for this reason that it disturbs the splendid order of classic scenography. It points itself out as a *fragment* which broaches the *unity* of the view, and consequently threatens the subject (=the spectator) who, literally, loses his way. However true it may be on the whole, such a theory still sidesteps the privilege of the figure, and above all does not explain what it has in common with others: a close-up is still a shot. And works which are deliberately based on fragmentation and explosion are not deprived of other forms: Vertov's films contain more than simply close-ups. This means that 'fragment' is insufficient as explanation.

We should like to attempt to analyse this vacillation, this fascinating difficulty, by way of an example: several works, several fragments of works by Josef von Sternberg. An impassioned creator — putting passion itself onstage — and fascinating for being of an extreme individuality in Hollywood production. Sternberg's affected indifference toward his material is belied by the resemblances among his films, and he himself at least is comprehensible in the twisting of this material, which he explores at will. Claude Ollier has aptly noted 'the exiguousness of the fields of operation to which Sternberg confines himself and in which he takes pleasure', and his willingness to constitute these fields in the 'laboratory'. He is interesting for this reason, because he develops what one could call a close-up way of seeing [*vision en gros plan*], giving to this expression the sense of a function which Eisenstein assigned, among others, to the figure of the close-up: metonymic representation.

Sternbergian space is always that of a universe under constraint, of which the exiguousness itself is exuberant, since its signs never cease to proliferate and refer to a multiple otherness. An otherness that might be purely conventional — a theatrical Spain or mythical China, simple sets for a fabulous mental theatre — but which owes all its reality to a permanent indexical invention or eruption. This metonymic process does not affect the image alone; it is well known that Sternberg is, with Lang, one of the greatest deployers of sound, in which he discerned the most realistic element: the suggestion of space in *The Blue Angel* is unequalled in this respect.

One imagines, then, that the true close-up partakes of a singular logic, and that it assumes its value quite as much, sometimes, from other shots as from itself; it is necessary to ponder its upsurge in particular, and understand the possibility or the necessity of the *passage* to this form, which determines its rarity as well as its frequency.

THE CURLING IRON

The Blue Angel, for example, contains only about ten close-ups, almost all of them located toward the end of the film, with the exception of the recurrent image of the animated clock-face, the carillon of which chimes out a song of Duty (honesty and loyalty) which ironically emphasises the fall of Professor Rath. On the other hand, the film abounds in medium shots and medium long shots, indices of *consolidation*; compared with full shots, which instil or maintain distance and order, they permit displacements, mutations which inwardly transform themselves, they change proximity into promiscuity: mixture and confusion usher in perversion and ruin. Even certain long shots (such as the audience in the cabaret) are treated as an overlapping of medium shots and medium long shots: zones of light and shade slice across bodies, while a proliferation of objects cuts up the space, refusing it any depth, thus mingling the protagonists in a common destiny.

The first real close-up of the film is, of course, the image of the curling iron that Jannings applies to the pages of a calendar in order to cool it: the pages burn and slowly twist away. It has a multiple function: syntactic in the first place since it precipitates the drama through the density of time in the manner of a dissolve. Its symbolic value, both metaphoric and metonymic, is too obvious to be insisted upon. But the image of this ancient appliance in which the years are consumed by flame is almost immediately followed by a near close-up: a mirror reflects for us the face of Jannings as he makes up — the egg is this time visible on his nose; his eyelids are heavy and black; his look is blank. And the other close-ups to come will yet connote solitude and abandonment. Moral decay is born in confusion, which has permitted its *capture*. Thus the rigorous relationship of the shots refines the space of the drama.

A CHINESE REVERIE

While the train pursues its course through the Chinese night, Shanghai Lily returns to her compartment. A medium, frontal shot of the room, plunged into shadow. The door opens, the area of light outlines a dark silhouette, of which the face *alone* is clearer, indicating its near-autonomy. The shadow of Marlene then closes the door behind her, throwing the room back into its original gloom, and obscuring her step toward us. The close-up arises in a perfect match, the motion of the actress having prepared the way to this luminous isolation of the face, that it might finally be given to our contemplation: an anxious and nostalgic meditation in which are felt the grip of memory and the disappointment of the present. The normality of the movement articulating the passage from the medium shot to the close-up, in its relation to the progress of the train (which will lead to the end of the separation), is the index of this *suspense* which submerges the reflection that has been ours to see. An interior world is evoked, which opens an abetting space. Such an analysis might seem a classic effect; but the originality of Sternberg is, it might be said, in preparing the reaction, the *jouissance*, by showing how — how much — the close-up was inscribed as possible in the preceding shot. That it is still a matter here of a fascinating face, and that the face has always been the permitted figure of the close-up, the summit and summation of the human body, which is not mutilated by it, changes very little in the matter. The simple ruse of a great manipulator. The elision of the body certainly reinvests the purity of the subject — think of the 'moral' of the film: confidence as the foundation of love — but it also prepares the way for this other close-up: the mute fervour of the hands pressed together in the night.

Such forms are then not inscribed in a register of utter disruption; rather they are the manifestations of latent presences. Doubtless because in its largest dimension space is differently organised, or can be fundamentally disoriented in relation to a look which desires to master it and appropriate it. This can be seen better with an example from *The Scarlet Empress*.

THE MARRIAGE OF CATHERINE

It is in Kazan Cathedral that Sophia-Catherine marries Peter, the Grand Duke of Russia. Such a subject, emphatically announced by an introductory title, evokes *a priori* something in the grand manner of Hollywood, of which the analogy in painting might be David's *Sacre*: a homogeneous space, bright and luminous, hierarchical, roles distributed among the players, with a prevailing order. Sternberg will refuse such a tactic, and prefer a more shadowy unity, substituting for the conventional space of a geometrical view a mental and ideal locality the paradox of which is that it arises from objects and even bodies, like the thousand eyes of a spectacle. A summary description of the 29 shots of the sequence should give an idea of it:[1]

1. Long shot (LS). Candles, bright lights, masses of lamps. Priests. Icons. Camera moves back and up, looking slightly downward. Liturgical chants rise while the camera tracks left.
2. Medium shot (MS). Priests, icons, candlesticks.

3. MS. A censer is swung behind a transparent veil beyond which the bride and groom appear, like shadows, advancing toward the left, holding candles.
4. MS as 2. Priests, candlesticks, raised staffs.
5. MS. Priests. Censer in the foreground.
6. MS. Priests holding crosses.
7. Leftward pan of the priests toward the cross.
8. MS. Icons, crosses.
9. MS. Priests, candles.
10. Medium long shot (MLS). Catherine and Peter, beside a tall candle.
11. MS. Priests, candles.
12. Close-up (CU). Slightly oblique. Catherine taking communion, beneath a veil.
13. CU. Peter takes communion in his turn, and smiles while chewing.
14. MLS. The Empress Elizabeth, holding a candle.
15. CU. Catherine's face from the front, a bewildered look beneath her veil.
16. CU. Alexei, irritated, alone.
17. CU. Catherine (as 15).
18. Big CU. The face of Alexei.
19. Extreme CU (ECU). The face of Catherine, near the flame of the candle. Her look is bewildered and agitated. (Long take: 13 sec.)
20. CU. The face of Alexei (as 18).
21. CU as 17. The face of Catherine, who raises her eyes while the flame continues to waver fitfully. The chants stop. Silence.
22. CU. Alexei (as 20). The chanting begins again.
23. LS. Candles, priests, icons, crosses. (Long take.)
24. Very extreme CU. The eyes of Catherine near the flame. The chanting is very loud. (Long take: 21 sec.)
25. MS. Catherine raises her wedding veil.
26. Big CU. The face of Peter, laughing as he turns his head. Chanting.
27. MLS slightly tilted up. The Empress.
28. CU. The hands of the bride and groom are linked; the ring. A veil is tied around the hands.
29. LS. Candles, priests. The camera tracks to the right, then moves up by tracking forward and up, ending on the Empress, from below, and the nine-branched candlestick, to her left. Very loud music. Fade out. This last movement of the camera is exactly the inverse of the movement described in the first shot of the sequence.

Such an enumeration, however tiresome, is nevertheless necessary in order to illuminate the essentially *rhythmic* value of this sequence in which there occur privileged moments which are peaks of the drama. It should be emphasised immediately, in order better to grasp the differential elements, that the profoundly *experienced* unity of the place is not that of a *represented* space, which here is given, wilfully disjoint; it is however produced by a series of convergent means. Note in the first place the perfect symmetry of shots 1 and 29, which encompass and link the ensemble of the scene, by exactly inverse camera movements. The obvious recurrence of similar elements — the repetition of the white silhouettes of the priests, the multifarious bristling of the staffs and crosses, the omnipresence of burning light, outsize candlesticks, candle flames — produces the identity of a space which representation has fragmented, and which is never offered to the fullness of an encompassing look. Whatever their respective sizes, the different shots, thanks to their accumulation of detail, present the same 'density', the same coefficient of occupation, which, in denying too great a depth to the space, assures each of them a flat homogeneity, an equal opacity. But the greatest factor of unity is without doubt a *non-visual* element: the sound, chanting and music, which accompanies the whole sequence, with the notable exception of one close-up (Shot 21). At this point which, subtly, does not coincide with the most intense moments (Shots 19 and, especially, 24), the look of Catherine fills the screen, her eyes roll back and turn toward heaven while the candle flame shudders and lets us read the solitude and utter despair of one who has been bound over and betrayed. With the view of Alexei, the accomplice of power but the victim of love, the chanting begins anew and is triumphantly accentuated, before returning again to the immense, panicked look (Shot 24). These extreme facial close-ups, the duration of which progressively increases so as to attain a fascinating, fantastic excess, result in no other space than that of a dreadful, dreamed scene, a purely imaginary place: looks can only slip away from one another, they are lost, not exchanged, and they remain isolated. And despite the powerful counterpoint of Shots 23 and 24, which oppose the eyes of Catherine to the shimmering mass of a large segment of the assembled spectators, these close-ups are fundamentally *not* the effects of breaking up an established homogeneity, for fragmentation, as we have seen, is the very principle of the composition. Close-ups do not function except as pure *intensities*, particles of a spectacle that fascinates in *all* its aspects, like a solar Argus. That the point of major incandescence, the central blaze, is the face of a woman, whose breath troubles without extinguishing an incessant flame, is but the confession of the director, for whom the look of the World became confused one day with the eyes of Marlene.

But this look, this face, this distracted character, yet weak and wounded, are captured here in canvas, every aspect of which is alight, and among which there reigns the silent image of power, the Empress, upon whom the sequence closes and dissolves away.

The figure of the close-up is rare in *The Blue Angel*, relatively restricted in *The Scarlet Empress*; it literally abounds in *The Shanghai Gesture*, which will be the final example. Here close-ups are almost always of faces, but Sternberg's display of them differs progressively and perceptibly from the classic and banal usage that he still adopts — in simple shot-reverse-shots — in a film such as *The Devil is a Woman*. Two things should be said. The first bears upon the systematic quality of their usage. The close-up focuses the gaze of the spectator on the look that is isolated. So long as this look is the appropriate sighting of an off-screen point, it confirms a process of perspective which seems therefore justified and is felt to refer to a point of view, even if there is no absolute identity between image and view (what would be called for by a strict 'subjective shot'). This type of close-up thus plays at the diegetic level the role of what Jakobson calls the 'shifter', substituting or adding another level of enunciation in relation to a first enunciation felt to be 'objective'. This reversal of classic usage, the close-up being used to *organise* the scenography systematically, is doubled, especially at the end of the film, by a second, more fundamental aspect, which fits into the general schema of this interpretation. The faces of *The Shanghai Gesture* are progressively revealed to be *masks*, the truth of which must be sought for beyond them, in the enigmatically glittering eyes. Once the drama is over they take their places in faces more sinister and grimacing than those of Carnival. Waiting for their gathering, they demand all our attention, fascinate our eye like the facets of a reality that is foreign to us. Their names are themselves deceptive: Gin Sling, mistress of pleasure and of gambling, of the painted face, the long, drawn-in eyelashes, the white forehead crowned by a cunning coiffure, strange and artificial; Sir Guy Charteris, of the European mask, the enterprising smile, the ignoble past. His daughter (Gene Tierney), with the turned up nose of an insolent, greedy child, whose features come apart, hairdo tumbles down, cheeks swell up. A few confederates accompany this trio slowly toward a mortal finale, following a prodigious dinner-party. The film's originality lies in Sternberg's competence in articulating a whole dialectic of look and of mask, soliciting our eye alternatively by the delicacy of the flesh, and by whatever lies beyond that which it desires to contemplate.

In alluding to Sternberg, it has been intended to exemplify, through several privileged moments of his work, a tension which appears to reverse a classic usage of the close-up, disclosing the power and the privilege of the figure while referring to the fundamental power of the cinema. The close-up is utilised as pure intensity, a differential mark raised up on a general opacity. This function is accomplished by a representation of space which breaks with an optical, geometrical structuration, one organised by a Subject in control of his Vision. Sternberg attempts, to the contrary, to restore to the represented world its ambiguous, variable nature, its luminous points, its radiant foci, its multiple, flashing sources of reflection; that is, according to Lacan's formula, 'that look which surrounds us, but which is not shown to us', that makes of the world an omni-voyeur. The waking state is characterised precisely by this elision of the look, elision of the fact that 'it looks and that it shows'. Inversely, in the dream, 'it shows', and our position, in dream activity, is basically to be the one who does not see.[2]

Now, what is the space of a dream if not the absence of an horizon, closure, emergence, contrast, staining, intensification? All characteristics which are those of Sternberg's cinema. A dream more intense than sight since it restores the density and the flash of the look.

(translated by Peter Baxter)

Notes

1. Editor's note: it should be pointed out that Audibert's summary of the sequence is incorrect in several details, perhaps most importantly in the last one numbered: while the camera does indeed track back toward the position of Empress Elizabeth, that shot cuts to a low-angle medium close shot of the exultant monarch. The sequence is not so neatly framed as Audibert would have it, but in being gathered to the overwhelming 'look' of dominance, which is not that of a space, the point he is making seems even more pertinent.

2. Audibert is quoting, roughly, from Jacques Lacan, *Les quatre concepts fondamentaux de la psychanalyse* (Paris; Editions du Seuil, 1973), pp. 71-72.

BARRY SALT

Sternberg's Heart Beats in Black and White

Where does it beat? In the centre of the frame. How does it beat? Slowly. Is this just rhetorical hyperbole? No, I will explain.

Here are four sequences of frame enlargements taken from *The Scarlet Empress*. If you look carefully at those in Sequence I, taken at a fixed interval of 160 frames (6.7 seconds), you can see that they show a regular alternation between mainly light and mainly dark tones in the centre of the frame, from one frame to the next. This slow pulsing or flow of light and dark through the centre of the frame is achieved in a number of different ways in this and in other films made by von Sternberg in the thirties. Sometimes the simple change from one shot to the next reverses the basic tonality in the central area, as in the first eight frames illustrated, which make up a montage sequence following the title 'Across a huge soft carpet of snow . . .' and also frames 24, 25, 26 which intersect more or less static shots. But mostly these large changes in tonality of the image in the central area are produced by movements within the frame resulting from camera and/or actor movements. In frames 9-14, which all fall within the length of one longish take lasting 33 seconds, the changes from light to dark are produced by groups of horsemen in alternately light and dark coats riding up through the frame from the bottom to the top. This use of the movement of actors either in very light or very dark costumes through the centre of the frame is in fact the principal way the pulsation from light to dark is achieved in Sternberg's thirties films, and many other examples of it can be seen in the other illustrated sequences (e.g., shots illustrated by the groups of frames in Sequence II, 1-4 and 17-22 and Sequence III, 2-6 and 7-10).

After the shot just described in Sequence I come three short shots, only one of which is intersected by the 160 frame division being used (15), and then another longish take running over frames 16-20 in which the dark chandelier forms one of the dark patches flowing through the frame. (Here and elsewhere Sternberg is the first and only director to get any use out of *dark* chandeliers and lamps.) Subsequent shots in this sequence are covered by the groups of frames 21-23, 24, 25,26-27, 28, 29,

103

30-31, 32, 33, 34-35, 36.

The steady rhythmic pattern I have described continues through several more shots which are not reproduced, until a very short dissolve introduces what is more or less a direct continuation of the same scene, and at this point I resume the illustrations, as Sequence II, with the same 160 frame interval between them. Straightaway we have another long take covered by the first four frame enlargements of a miniature procession through a doorway by characters attired in alternately light and dark clothes who appear in succession in the centre of the frame. After 9 more frames, corresponding to 7 shots through which the processes already described continue, the tempo of the rhythmic pulsation of light and dark in the centre of the frame doubles, and to show this the frame illustrations from number 14 are taken once every 80 frames.

It is also in this sequence that actual shadow, as opposed to naturally dark costumes and objects, plays a part in producing the dark patches passing through the centre of the frame. This can be seen for instance at frame number 34 in the illustrations. In general actual shadow plays a small part compared with the darkness of black costumes and objects in generating the apparent strong chiaroscuro of Sternberg's images, and indeed many of his scenes that appear to be made up of strong contrasts of light and dark areas are actually lit with high key lighting — the lighting is uniformly bright over the whole picture area — as can be seen by careful examination of all the frame stills collected here. This feature of Sternberg's approach to the static image, which was quite conscious, became more pronounced as the thirties wore on, but it was apparently not understood by his associates. For instance, Lee Garmes has posthumously rebuked him for not understanding the 'necessity' to have an equal distribution of light and shadow in the image — meaning of course actual shadow, which is what cameramen are ordinarily concerned in producing and manipulating to get photographic effects.

It might be wondered if these regular rhythms in the picture have some connection with regularities in the music track, but this cannot be, for the scenes illustrated by the frame enlargements are largely unaccompanied by music. In the first section shown, the background music which accompanies the initial montage sequence stops shortly after the beginning of the next scene of the arrival at the Russian court, and similarly for Sequence III following the title 'From the very start . . .' In fact if we examine carefully the musical accompaniment to the montage sequence after 'Across a huge soft carpet of snow . . .' we find that it is just a succession of popular classical themes with no particular *musical* connection with one another; a kind of crude collage without the kind of musically smooth transitions we usually find in like cases in other Hollywood films.

> *Mea culpa*; **I had not left much for others to do, even being bold enough to conduct the members of the Los Angeles Symphony orchestra in playing the background music.**
>
> **Josef von Sternberg**

Just so. And even in the wedding scene, which has a continuous music track alone, the relation of the musical phrases to the action is very slight except at the very beginning and end of the scene, and it has none at all that I can see to the regular pulsation of light and dark at centre frame.

In the wedding scene the period of pulsation is again 160 frames, and something similar seems to apply to most of the film, though Sequence III which covers the two earlier scenes following the title 'From the very start . . .' has a basic pulsation of 127 frames (5.3 seconds). Consequently the frame enlargements are taken at that interval throughout the two scenes which end with the title 'After weeks of hard riding . . .' There are no sections of double tempo pulsation in these two scenes.

Another point of some interest is raised by Sequence III at frame enlargements 20 and 25, in which the replacement of a light area by a dark area in the centre of the image is produced by Count Alexei leaning in front of Sophia Frederica and kissing her. This is one of the rare points where the visual process I have been describing can be reasonably considered to have some degree of expressive function, namely underlining visually the submission of Sophia Frederica to Count Alexei. At a few other places in this film, and also in others by Sternberg, he makes a characteristic expressive use of shadow over the face or eyes of one of his characters when they might be assumed to be feeling confused or unhappy or uncertain. Just such an instance is illustrated from near the beginning of the film when Sophia Frederica first meets Count Alexei (Sequence IV). However, in even these limited number of cases — several per film — the information available usually makes it slightly uncertain exactly which of these emotions the character might be feeling, and again there is further ambiguity in meaning from case to case. After all, unhappiness is not the same as uncertainty. Beyond these few cases, as far as I can see the flow of dark and light in Sternberg's films has no meaning in any real sense of the word, though those hell-bent on producing interpretations at any cost could no doubt invent some. Just as one can see camels in the clouds and continents in cracks on the wall if one wants to.

> **As if I were a computing machine, I built scene after scene to form an exact pattern . . .**
>
> **Josef von Sternberg**

So this statement is the literal truth rather than rhetorical exaggeration as one might at first (or even at second) think? Well, not quite, for my analysis has simplified what is actually going on in *The Scarlet Empress* a little. The sharp-eyed will have noted that there are one or two stutters in the rhythm of the pulsation of black and white as I have illustrated it here, and beyond that the period of the pulsation is not quite completely steady at 160 frames or 127 frames, as the case might be. In fact the period of alternation fluctuates around these values, but hardly ever gets far enough away for successive black phases and white phases to escape the grid I have laid upon them. Even this much is in itself quite remarkable and unique.

Then of course there are the short sections of double tempo pulsations in some scenes which I have already mentioned, and finally it must be said that there are a few short scenes, forming a very minor part of its length, in which the process is totally in abeyance, and the centre of the frame remains light in tone throughout. One such is the scene in which the Grand Duchess makes the servants take the places of the court at the dinner table.

But the best way to appreciate this temporo-visual structure in *The Scarlet Empress* and the other Sternberg-Dietrich films is to run them backwards and forwards at high speed on a viewing machine with the central circular area marked on the screen. Or failing that, the next time one of the films is shown on television, draw a circle with a fibre-tipped pen on the tube, sit back, and marvel.

A few people have had intimations of the kinetic-visual effect you will see, but they have never grasped it in its completeness. For instance Aeneas Mackenzie in his celebrated article 'Leonardo of the Lenses' has it that Sternberg obtains his effects purely by movement within the shot, and that this alone propels the drama, whereas I have shown that cutting from one shot to the next also plays its part at times in the pulsation of light and dark, and also that in the main all this proceeds quite independently of the dramatic developments, and indeed is anti-dramatic in its regular alternation.

> **. . . a film is built out of a succession of mobile images, each replacing the last, though their cumulative effect can be as powerful as the impact of a single canvas, providing that the shifting values are controlled to produce a homogeneous entity.**
> **Josef von Sternberg**

True indeed, and we have just seen the major way that the shifting values produce the homogeneous entity, but some other visual shifts remain to be noted.

Although most of Sternberg's compositions have strong central organization, as is usually the case in mainstream cinema, he does vary this occasionally with a diptych type of static composition. Mostly this vertical central division of the frame is only implied, as in Sequence III, frame 12, with a light coloured vertical figure in the left half of the frame, and a dark one filling the right half, but on rare occasions some foreground object in the set produces an actual vertical line dividing the screen in two halves. There are no examples of this in the illustrations here, but the shadowed statue holding up a crucifix in frame 21 of Sequence I goes halfway to dividing the frame in this way. Incidentally this distorted Russian Orthodox cross is a recurring element at the centre of the frame of this film, and it increases in size throughout, until at the end it rises the full height of the frame, while Tsar Peter is strangled behind it. This image is simultaneously another of the continuing series in Sternberg's work that owes something to the drawings of Felicien Rops, as does the earlier one of a man hung by his feet from the clapper of a bell, and the later one of Catherine signalling her assumption of power by pulling on a bell rope. (Compare Rops' *Le Vrille.*) But this side of Sternberg's films does not concern me at the moment, fascinating though it is. I must return to the abstract patterns of visual organization in *The Scarlet Empress* and the other films.

Although *The Scarlet Empress* and *The Devil is a Woman* show this regular pulsation of light and dark in the centre of the frame in its most fully developed form, it is already well established in *Der Blaue Engel*, occurring in about half the scenes, while in *Morocco* it is nearly continuous, though with the middle grey of the legionnaires' uniforms sometimes forming a third term in the alternation along with the usual black and white. Before that the process is still struggling to reveal itself, and when one goes back to *Underworld* it only exists inside single shots, and obviously has no rhythmic regularity. At that initial stage Sternberg was experimenting with the looming shadows of moving people passing across brightly lit wall areas, and it is doubtful if he had discovered what could be done with the alternation of light and dark costumes, but *Underworld* certainly contains one instance of the control of light by painting the décor. When Bull Weed escapes from prison his dark figure creeps past a fairly brightly lit grey wall at the centre of a darkish image, and the brightness of the centre is accentuated by having an irregular splodge of white paint slapped on it. A certain connection with the practices of the German set designers of *Der Letzte Mann*, etc., springs to mind here. (See Barry Salt, 'From Caligari to Who?', *Sight & Sound*, Vol. 48, No. 2, pp. 119-123.)

And also like those earlier Murnau films which were so dominated by pre-production design of the shots, Sternberg's films rarely repeat a camera set-up in the chain of shots as edited. In the process of making a considerable change of the image from one shot to the next, he nearly always changed the closeness or scale of shot from one to the next, moving continuously back and forth equally over nearly the whole range of possible scale of shot.

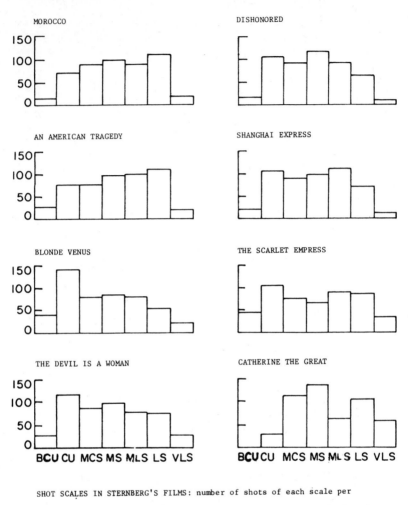

SHOT SCALES IN STERNBERG'S FILMS: number of shots of each scale per 500 shots (comparison provided with Paul Czinner's Catherine the Great).

Throughout his career, Sternberg made fairly equal use of closenesses or scales of shot from Close-Up (showing head and shoulders) to Medium Close Shot (with the figure from waist to head reaching the height of the frame) through Medium Shot (hips upward) and Medium Long Shot (knees to head reaching the height of the frame) to Long Shot (showing the full height of the body). Big Close-Ups, which show just the head, and Very Long Shots always played a much smaller part in the scheme of his shots. This would seem to be because it is much more difficult to produce variety in the patterns of light and dark in the image at these two extremes by the methods Sternberg ordinarily used. The degree of constancy Sternberg achieved in respect of his use of the different scales of shot throughout his career is best illustrated with bar charts showing the number of shots of each scale of shot or closeness of shot in 500 shots Sternberg used in each of his Paramount Dietrich films. For comparative purposes the like figures are illustrated for Paul Czinner's *Catherine the Great* (1934). The distinctiveness of the distribution of shots amongst the different possible scales of shot in Sternberg's films can be seen by comparison with those for other varied films given in Barry Salt, 'Statistical Style Analysis of Motion Pictures', *Film Quarterly*, Vol. 28, No. 1, pp. 13-22, where the method was first introduced. Suffice it to say that Czinner's film on the same subject as *The Scarlet Empress* has considerably greater emphasis on the use of more distant shots, as you can see, while some other directors of the thirties stayed even further back from the action, and then again yet others used a far greater proportion of close shots than Sternberg.

One can also see from the bar charts that at the beginning of the thirties Sternberg himself was very slightly more inclined to use more distant shots than he was in the silent period or from 1933 onwards. This deviation is a result of the technical constraints on the shooting of early sound films, either having to use cameras in large soundproof booths, as in *Der Blaue Engel*, or with inadequately soundproofed blimps and inefficient microphones as in *Morocco*. Although the restriction on close shooting was not absolute, both kinds of technical shortcomings produced a mild pressure to keep the camera back from the actors which you see reflected in these shot distributions. When these difficulties were overcome, Sternberg was free to return to something very close to his silent period approach in this respect.

Another manifestation of technical pressures on the early sound film can be seen in the differing types of transitions Sternberg used between scenes in his early thirties films. This feature is the subject of a statistical analysis by Lawrence Benaquist given in a paper, 'A Syntagmatic and Punctuational Analysis of Josef von Sternberg's Films, 1928-1941', delivered at the Purdue Film Conference in 1978. Benaquist found that between *Thunderbolt* and *The Scarlet Empress* the number of scene transitions made with fades decreased from 12 to 1 or 2, while at the same time the number of dissolves rose from 3 to nearly 100. This is a reflection of the fact that a dissolve between shots taken with synchronous sound mostly requires an accompanying mix (cross-fade) on the sound track to be made after editing, with another stage of sound re-recording. Up until the middle of 1931 this re-recording of the sound onto a new optical sound film audibly increased the level of noise and distortion on the new combined sound track, so this procedure was avoided if possible, and hence the use of dissolves in the picture was avoided too. In Sternberg's films the transition to the free use of dissolves occurs between *Dishonored* and *An American Tragedy.* Once it became easy and convenient to make dissolves at the editing stage, Sternberg occasionally used them to make small adjustments to the rhythm within a shot or to juxtapose two shots that he had not originally planned to use in that way, and an example of this can be seen in the actual film of *The Scarlet Empress* immediately before the title 'Across a huge soft carpet of snow. . .' His preplanning of his films was not perfect, merely almost perfect.

. . . I paid a final tribute to the lady I had seen lean against the wings of a Berlin stage.

Josef von Sternberg

Can the value of such a tribute be counted? In this case, the answer is yes. If we count the shots of Marlene Dietrich in *The Scarlet Empress* in which it can be seen, both in the shot itself, and from the two surrounding shots, that no one is definitely looking at her, and compare this with the number of those shots in which it is clear that some one in the film is looking at her, we find that there are 40 of the former and 72 of the latter.

The point of these figures only becomes clear when we compare them with those for an almost contemporary film on the same subject, *Catherine the Great,* which was created by Paul Czinner as a star vehicle for his wife, Elizabeth Bergner, in the same name part. In this film there are 93 shots of the Empress in which it is clear that people are looking at her, and only 17 in which they are not. The significance of this manner of presentation of Dietrich in the Sternberg film is fully established if we look back at earlier films in the series. In *Morocco* there are 54 shots of Dietrich in which it is apparent that people are looking at her, and 32 in which they are not, while in *Der Blaue Engel* the respective figures are 34 and 16. However, if we look back past the Dietrich films to *Underworld,* in which Evelyn Brent plays the female lead, we find that there is a marked change in the proportions of these two kinds of shots, towards values that seem more characteristic of the conventional treatment of a female star, for there are 52 shots in which some one is looking at her, and only 14 in which no one is. But if we look at the shots in which the male lead of *Underworld,* George Bancroft, is alone in the frame, with people looking at him or not looking at him, as the case may be, we find 62 of the former, and 52 of the latter. This high figure immediately suggests that in this film George Bancroft in some sense takes the Dietrich role, and although specific figures are not at the moment available for the other Sternberg films from before 1930, memory suggests that the presentation of the male lead in isolation is characteristic of them too.

My conclusion is that the pre-Dietrich films are structurally different from those with Dietrich in the presentation of the female lead, as well as in the kinetic treatment of light and dark, and that there is strong objective evidence for this, although some writers such as Andrew Sarris have suggested the contrary. Sternberg's 'filtered feminine mystique' took a back seat in his films before the advent of Marlene Dietrich. (Nevertheless, Andrew Sarris's comments on the general thematics of von Sternberg's work are in a class of their own, in part because they are based on the known facts about von Sternberg and his opinions and ideas of what he was doing, rather than being the usual baseless speculations of interpretation.)

The work of an artist communicates the calibre of his thinking, not the calibre of his emotions, though the latter does not interfere when under control.

Josef von Sternberg

And what are we to say of the artist who organized the details I have described, not to mention the hundreds of more obvious ones in his films? Might not some special descriptive category be useful to contain him? Could we call it 'genius', or is that word too offensive to the untalented?

The field of art is vast ... and no scale, calibration, or test tube can aid in its analysis.

Josef von Sternberg

Even a genius can be wrong sometimes.

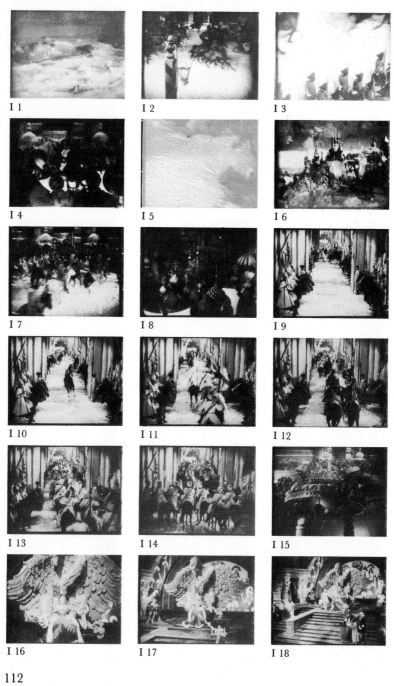

I 1

I 2

I 3

I 4

I 5

I 6

I 7

I 8

I 9

I 10

I 11

I 12

I 13

I 14

I 15

I 16

I 17

I 18

I 19

I 20

I 21

I 22

I 23

I 24

I 25

I 26

I 27

I 28

I 29

I 30

I 31

I 32

I 33

I 34

I 35

I 36

II 1

II 2

II 3

II 4

II 5

II 6

II 7

II 8

II 9

II 10

II 11

II 12

II 13

II 14

II 15

II 16

II 17

II 18

114

II 19

II 20

II 21

II 22

II 23

II 24

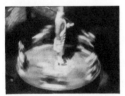
II 25

II 26

II 27

II 28

II 29

II 30

II 31

II 32

II 33

II 34

II 35

II 36

115

III 1

III 2

III 3

III 4

III 5

III 6

III 7

III 8

III 9

III 10

III 11

III 12

III 13

III 14

III 15

III 16

III 17

III 18

III 19   III 20   III 21

III 22   III 23   III 24

III 25   III 26   III 27

III 28   III 29   III 30

After weeks of hard riding the Russian border was reached, where the populace hid behind closed shutters — out of the way of the feared Cossacks, who with reckless fury protected their nobles from even a glance of the enslaved people.

III 31   III 32   III 33

IV 1

IV 2

IV 3

IV 4

IV 5

IV 6

BLAINE ALLAN

The Only Voice in the World: Telling *The Saga of Anatahan*

The story of Anatahan is a true story that out-Hollywoods Holly-wood.[1]

I

In the Sternberg canon, *The Saga of Anatahan* has held a privileged position. The circumstances surrounding the film's production appear to indicate that it is an ideal, finally-realized, from which all previous Sternberg films might have sprung. Thousands of miles from the constraints of Hollywood, the director had two sympathetic producers.[2] Having once constructed the Moroccan desert on the Paramount back lot, Sternberg would now build a tropical island to his own specifications within the walls of a studio. His Japanese producers, however, did not have the means of Paramount in the 1930s. In fact, the studio in which Sternberg was to produce *Anatahan* had once been an airplane hangar, and most recently an industrial exhibition hall. In addition, of course, this was to be Sternberg's last movie, and might be thought of as his swan song, and an encapsulation of the themes, motifs, and stylistic elements which comprise the Sternberg text.

However, among all his films, Sternberg acknowledges that *Anatahan* was his 'most unsuccessful'.[3] Sternberg clearly sees the failure of the film not in terms of the adequate or inadequate realization of a dream-project, but in its reception, and in the relations between the film and its viewers. He measures critical reception as he concludes his own account of *Anatahan* with a summary of the film's poor reception in Japan, its few distribution outlets in the U.S.A., and the mutilation of the sound track in Great Britain. He finishes, however, on a more hopeful note by quoting at length from Philippe Demonsablon's laudatory review in *Cahiers du Cinéma*.

In a sense, though, Sternberg's real conclusions on the project are to be found at the start, rather than the end, of his tale, and they are almost

119

serene in attempting to account for the film's failure. He writes:

> There are two minor factors equally decisive in the destiny of a film,
> one being proper circulating outlets and the other the time in which
> the work appears. To be ahead of the times is not much better than to
> be behind, and often worse.[4]

As befits a filmmaker who spent most of his working life within the
industrial structures of Hollywood, one eye is pointed towards getting
the film into the public circuit, while the other takes a second glance at
the material to see that it corresponds with the public tenor. Evidently,
Sternberg found fault with *Anatahan* on both counts.

Though *Anatahan* is in one sense a war film, it takes place on the
periphery of the Second World War's Pacific theatre. In 1944, a
Japanese shipping convoy is shelled off the coast of the small island of
Anatahan. The shipwrecked men — most of them merchant rather than
military sailors — find their way ashore. There they discover the few
remaining residents of the island, including Keiko, the only woman left,
and Kusakabe. He is initially assumed to be her husband, though both
their spouses have already left the island. They all establish a
community in their isolated setting, and remain there for seven years,
well past the Japanese surrender in 1945 and the end of the war. By the
time they are rescued and taken off Anatahan, where they have all
competed for power and dominance, five of the men have been killed.

Criticism has generally recognized Sternberg's films on one level for
their visual style, and on another for their treatment of, and appeal to,
emotion. Andrew Sarris welcomes Sternberg into his directors' Panth-
eon, proclaiming that he 'became a lyricist of light and shadow rather
than a master of montage. The control he achieved over his studio
surroundings encouraged him to concentrate on the spatial integrity of
his images rather than on their metaphorical juxtaposition.'[5] Sarris goes
on to discover thematic ends in 'emotional autobiography' or 'personal
fantasies' rather than in universal allegory. John Baxter puts the concern
for emotion at the centre of his study. 'Under Sternberg's scrutiny', he
writes, 'a reality emerges that is at once obvious and infinitely complex in
its implications, the world of human emotion, of love and its dark
concomitant, the desire to destroy.'[6] Though the films are firmly rooted
in fiction, the literary correlative most often used in criticism of
Sternberg's work is poetry. Sarris makes the comparison in the quotation
above, and makes it even more explicit later in the essay. Raymond
Durgnat concludes an article on Sternberg with the words, 'Poetic
freedom is the mainspring of these wilful, glittering, delirious films',
thereby putting aspects of poetry at the conceptual centre of his
argument.[7]

The Saga of Anatahan afforded Sternberg the opportunity to indulge those elements which future critical writing would cite as having been essential across the body of his film work. With this in mind, it is perhaps perverse that a dominant element of the film is a spoken commentary, which runs throughout the picture. Such a commentary is uncommon in narrative fiction film, although *Anatahan's* use of the device is not unprecedented. There is, for instance, the notorious case of *Sunset Boulevard*. Narrated by a dead man, it will prove an apt comparison to *Anatahan*, as we shall see. The narration of *Jules et Jim* is nearly as insistent as that of *Anatahan*. Commentary, however, is quite foreign to most of Sternberg's films. On the most superficial level, it might be said that such a device works counter to an emphasis on visual style and emotional engagement and identification. What, then, are the effects and ramifications of a commentary, such as found in *Anatahan,* and what are its relations both to fiction-making processes and to the viewer?

II

In his book *Josef von Sternberg: A Critical Study*, Herman G. Weinberg prints a transcription of the narration for *The Saga of Anatahan*.[8] A tireless Sternberg champion, Weinberg might have rationalized its inclusion by reference to the director's personal authorship of the script and, moreover, to the fact that Sternberg himself speaks the narration on the film's sound track. The film's commentary is a central point of contention in discussions of the film. In pragmatic terms, for instance, John Baxter notes that the commentary appears initially to be an economical device, hedging against expensive, synchronized dialogue. On the other hand, he adds, synchronised dialogue actually shares the sound track with the commentary, a fact contradicting the assumption of cost-cutting.[9] Evaluating the prose itself, Andrew Sarris compares the commentary of this film to the titles for the silent film, *The Salvation Hunters*, and to Sternberg's memoirs, *Fun in a Chinese Laundry*. He faults Sternberg's 'addiction to overly abstract rhetoric and overly elegant turns of phrase'.[10]

Sarris seems on the mark in comparing *Anatahan's* commentary to the intertitles of the director's first film. On the surface, the spoken narration serves the same function as titles, introducing characters, translating dialogue (in this case from Japanese to English rather than from mute gesture to the printed word), and commenting upon action. The commentary also reinforces the possibility of seeing *Anatahan* as a Japanese film in addition to being a Sternberg film, in that it continues the tradition of the *benshi*. The *benshi* was a performer who provided live commentary or, in a sense, translation for the Japanese silent film audience. Sternberg's role parallels that of the *benshi* in several respects. They both assume voices for all characters in the film. Both, too, have acquired some degree of celebrity status for their performances.[11] While placing the commentary in this context, though, we must also confront the question of the place of this level of discourse within the text. Because the material is written and spoken by Sternberg, and because of the aura of the director's artistry, commentators such as Weinberg have let it rest as evidence of Sternberg's personal expression. In other words, the argument goes, while this personal expression may be divined in all the director's works, here it is made explicit and brought to the forefront for all to witness. Nevertheless, this particular element of the film can be read in relation to other, discrete aspects of the image and sound tracks, and in relation to comparable films.

In a sober and considered analysis of the film, Claude Ollier rightly sets the commentary in a clash with the Japanese dialogue and with the image itself:

> The English syllables are set against the 'foreign' sonority of the dialogue, which is never summarized, with one or two brief exceptions, and which the author characterizes as 'unimportant sound'. Then, the regular and parsimonious delivery, the even intonation, almost cold, indifferent, contrasts continually with the aggressiveness of the image, with the speech — 'harsh' for us — of the Japanese, and the vehemence of the music, which intensifies the chorus at each evocation of the native land.[12]

In his account, Ollier divides the sound track into the English commentary, Japanese dialogue (which is quite sparse), and music. The effects track must also be added to this. Though elegant, and laced with allusion and metaphor, the commentary is read in a voice, Sternberg's own, which is flat, detached, and ironic. There is no set formula for the relation between the English monologue and the Japanese dialogue. At times, the voice is indeed that of a translator, rendering the foreign dialogue in English, presumably verbatim, after the original is spoken. At other points, the commentary translates dialogue before it is spoken by the characters. Japanese speech, incomprehensible to the foreign viewer, is also permitted to carry meaning without the explicit benefit of translation, as in the case of Keiko's songs, or the extended quarrel between Keiko and Kusakabe. Here, the one language openly clashes with the other. While the English commentary indicates one type of audience, Japanese dialogue points to another. Implicitly, the English voice demands attention and, moreover, the listener must rely upon it for verbal information, unless that listener understands Japanese. Even so, the two discourses, set in the balance, are not evenly matched. For one thing, there is simply more of the English commentary than there is of Japanese dialogue. In addition, the role of the commentator as translator helps determine his position of dominance which is even more marked at the points when translation is absent. At those points, a gap interrupts the linguistic pathway into the film.

Nevertheless, while the voice is detached from the film's action, it is also complicit with it. Though the commentary is spoken in English, it is also the reminiscence of a participant in the Anatahan incident; furthermore, it is the voice of a survivor. However, it is fruitless to speculate which of the survivors passes his recollections on to us. The characteristics of the voice are telling, not only in terms of Sternberg's own vocal traits, but also with regard to the construction of the commentary text. Introducing the transcription, Weinberg writes, 'Inspired by an actual episode of the late war in the Pacific, and adapted by the director from a book on the subject written by one of the survivors of "the battle of Anatahan", the commentary is written, as is the book, in the first person.'[13] The first person is, of course, typical for writings in the form of memoirs. In pointing to the correspondence between the printed memoirs and the film, though, Weinberg suppresed the obvious difference. Not only is the commentary not written from the vantage point of a specific participant, but it scrupulously collects the characters together and speaks on their behalf as a group. Memoirs are written in the singular; *Anatahan* is spoken in the plural.

As the expression of memory, it is also a voice of recollection, and hence of reconstruction. The speaker tells us that they were not privy to certain events, such as the murder of Semba, the youngest sailor, in the swing. Thus the voice is required to rely on speculation ('We can only guess how he got into that hammock.'). Nor do any of the characters actually see, as we do, Keiko signal a passing ship, and walk into the sea to be returned safely to Japan. The voice, then, is in the place of the participants, within the fiction; it is also, however, in *our own place*, the place of the spectator. So, it speaks on behalf of the characters in the fiction, and it speaks on our behalf as well. As we are permitted to see Keiko's surrender, the commentator refers specifically to the events on the image track, noting laconically, 'We did not see this.'

III

The Saga of Anatahan is based primarily on the published recollections of Michiro Maruyama, one of the survivors of the Anatahan incident.[14] Sternberg's refusals to meet with Maruyama or Kazuko Higa, the woman who was rescued from the island in 1950, the real-life Keiko, are generally acknowledged only anecdotally.[15] This refusal or missed research opportunity, however, parallels the end result, the film text. The film's commentary is one of recollection, and also of homogeneous collectivity rather than one of individual personality. 'Recollection', too, is something of a misnomer. Instead, as the commentator tells us what they did or did not see, the mode is more literally 'looking back', setting the image in the past and the commentary in the present. The commentator, then, is in the process of seeing things which he has never seen before. In this way, the film proposes that what we *see* bears the weight of truth. In turn, this can be elaborated upon, and somewhat fleshed out by the perspective of the commentary, but not fully. In this structure, the commentary is the voice of discovery.

The narrative voice, however, is equivocal. The death of Yananuma, the usurper, at the hands of Kusakabe, the husband, follows the New Year's celebration. The narrator reads: 'At all this, too, no one else was present. We can only reconstruct the events from which we were barred. The King and Queen had left our festival — that we knew — but we never saw the King again. He had been marked for death, indelibly, long ago. The only thing we did not know was — who would be the executioner?'[16] Here, the narration bears numerous qualities and connotative shades: fate or destiny ('marked for death; indelibly'); justice and retribution, implying a firm morality ('the executioner'); metaphor ('the King and Queen').[17] The commentary's placement within the film, though, reinforces the prohibition and deferment referred to in the first two sentences of this passage. In fact, the second sentence, because it is set in the present tense, reads more or less as a platitude. We are informed that Yananuma's death is imminent, but it has not yet occurred on screen. The prohibition here is two-fold. As the narrator speaks these words, Yananuma and Keiko are embracing, alone in his hut. The rest of the men (our collective narrator) were barred from seeing this sexual event at the time. We, however, are permitted the sight which is denied even Kusakabe, the murderer. He stabs Yananuma, his successor, blindly, as Hamlet killed Polonius, through the wall of the foliage-covered hut. In this respect, we see what the participants cannot. In a case such as this one, the film affords us a privileged view which cannot be reconciled with any one character in the fiction. We and the narrative voice are accomplices; moreover, the narrative voice binds the action to the whole structure of the narrative.

A couple of significant breaks occur in the image/commentary structure. Both are signalled by incursions from outside the island. In both cases, the castaways are informed that the war is over, that Japan has surrendered to the Allies. The first time, of course, the Anatahan community believes the announcement to be an enemy ruse, and refuses to leave the island sanctuary. The second time the end of the war is announced, though, Keiko escapes and sends back letters from the island-dwellers' families to confirm the surrender and to draw them home.

This final sequence of the film, their homecoming, stands clearly in the realm of fantasy. The survivors return to an airstrip in Japan. They are greeted as 'heroes to all but ourselves', as the narrator says. The crowd that waits to greet them, though, is never seen, nor are the photographers whose flashbulbs pop before them. As Keiko watches, alone, not only do the living disembark from the plane, but so do the five victims of Anatahan. Each glides forward, toward the camera. Only here, at the end of the film, in the final line of narration, is the voice given individuality, or singular subjectivity.[18] The voice speaks, 'And if I know anything at all about Keiko — she too must have been there.' Even here, when the voice refers to itself individually, it is not anchored to any character in the image track. Each of the returning sailors is distinct from the others, as he moves through darkness and light in the frame. Similarly, Keiko is here not seen in the same shot as any of the other characters. The sequence is visually fragmented into shots of individuals, in contrast to the pattern of group shots of the castaways while they are isolated on the island.

The second break in the image/commentary structure is central to the film. Sternberg, it is reported, disliked the inclusion of war footage following the announcement of the surrender. For the production of *The Saga of Anatahan*, Sternberg constructed a detailed and graphic chart of the film's action, character relationships, narrative, and structure.[19] The sixteen characters are lined up at the top of the first page and traced vertically, downward, in a type of narrative flow chart. However, as none of the characters is directly involved in this particular sequence, it appears as a gap between sequences ten and eleven, which include the announcement of the surrender and the discovery of the wrecked airplane, respectively. In terms of the narrative, of course, this gap marks a turning point. The airplane carries culture as its cargo. From a piece of wire, the musician Maruyama (the name, recall, of the survivor historian of Anatahan, who was indeed a musician) constructs a samisen, his instrument. Keiko discovers a parachute, from which she makes gaily patterned garments. Young Semba finds a ring, the symbol of a legitimate marriage, just a few minutes in screen time after his attempt to intervene in Kusakabe's and Keiko's mock-marriage. Finally, Nishio and Yananuma uncover revolvers. Firearms are not totally new to the community at this point in the film. A machine gun had been rescued and brought ashore after the initial attack and wreck of the convoy. However, the gun is left on the shore, turned ever outward in order to protect the community as a whole. In addition, it is manned by the non-commissioned officer who has been ostracized by the merchant seamen as his notions of military discipline are rejected in favour of a new, civilian order. Unlike the machine gun, the sidearms are put into the hands of individuals, and it is here that power based on *possession* is made evident. 'Two old pistols', intones the narrator, '— two new masters.' In fact, the idea is extended overtly to Keiko, who leaves Kusakabe to go, as the narrator phrases it quite accurately, 'into circulation', like currency or commodities in an exchange system.

The gap between sequences ten and eleven is filled with stock footage. The film appears to have been taken from newsreels or documentary coverage of the surrender and demobilization at the immediate conclusion of the war. The photographic quality is different from that of most of the film. It is grainy and unpolished in contrast to the dense, pristine monochrome of the narrative sequences. Moreover, the sound quality is altered, removing sound effects and retaining only music and commentary tracks. These are elements which are constructed after the fact of the Anatahan incident, as far as the narrative voice of the film is concerned. They are events to which the castaways could not have had access at the time of the story. In fact, the island inhabitants actively denounce these events as untrue or fictitious. In effect, though, with the selection of these images and their combination and insertion into the structure of the film, the necessary notion of context and of history breaks through the veneer of allegory. For a few moments, fiction becomes documentary.

With this in mind, a brief comparison which might not otherwise have arisen would be instructive. Like Roberto Rossellini's *Paisà*, *Anatahan* is about the end of the Second World War. Sternberg's film is also very nearly as contemporaneous as the Italian film with its referent. The last survivors were removed from the Pacific island of Anatahan in mid-1951.[20] The film went into production little more than a year later. Both films explicitly locate their narratives in historical fact, and communicate that veracity by the same means. The six episodes of *Paisà* are punctuated with extra-diegetic material, mainly maps which chart the Allied invasion of Italy, from Sicily northward. Similarly, *Anatahan* commences with the attack on the supply convoy in 1944, superimposed over a revolving globe, which then dissolves into the image of a map of the island of Anatahan.

In terms of modes of discourse, both films combine documentary and expository elements on the one hand, and melodramatic narrative on the other. Both pictures concern the relation of the interpersonal to its broader and historical contexts. Yet, in this sense, the documentary, or exposition, is used to lend veracity to the melodramatic, to place the drama at a particular moment and place. The verbal sound track appropriates a dominant, organizing function over these sections of the films. Moving along a structural hierarchy, these expository elements, in their turn, organize the fiction in terms of an historical referent. Though, to be sure, the films are narrative in form, we may also look at them usefully in terms of recent work on the documentary film. Both films use the mode of direct address, a device which is typically associated with the documentary or instructional film. Moreover, both mix cinematic modes and overtly incorporate aspects of documentary and newsreel within their respective fictions.[21]

Paisà is comprised of a half-dozen, self-contained, short narratives. The nominally objective 'Voice of God' intervenes only at the head and tail of each, specifically in order to span the gap between sequences. The narrator describes the progress of Allied troops through Italy, while animated graphics illustrate the movement northward. Such a discourse provides an overt, geographical logic to the film as a whole. By providing such a logic for us, it also stems the impulse to construct other, deeper (historical or thematic, for example) logical structures which might serve to unify the discrete segments of the film.

In *Anatahan*, similar mechanisms are at work. Sternberg's film, however, is an extended narrative with one form of conventionalized unity. That narrative unity, though, is expressively *broken* by the documentary elements which work to lend the film historical veracity. In addition, the film is bound together by the voice of a collective witness to the incidents depicted on the image track. That perspective on the events is at once limited by the narrator's placement on the island, as a castaway, and broadened, in that the narration looks back and re-orders the events within a context.

In his article, Claude Ollier remarks on the constitution of the décor of the film, arguing that the jungle island setting is, in fact, constituted rather than *re*constituted from a referent external to the film. He continues: 'There exists a striking parallelism between the reduction, by abstraction, of space on the level of plot, and its compression by artifice on the level of the *mise-en-scène*. The two operations, with von Sternberg, are always closely connected.'[22] Spatially, then, the film fractures and reduces the setting of the island. It works from shot to shot, and does not provide an encompassing visual sense of the geography of the fictional world. Temporally, the film is equally reductive and elusive. Ellipses arise in the spaces between sequences. However, the narrator here performs a vital duty, and supplies an avenue which bypasses these transgressions of fictional unity. The narrator glosses over eruptions in the narrative surface, such as the insertion of the expository or documentary depicting a scene far away from the island inhabitants, or the transformation into fantasy — the 'ghosts' — at the film's conclusion.

Moreover, in so far as the narration is reflective, rewriting the story of the Battle of Anatahan yet again, it also determines a further diegetic plane which supersedes the image track. In *Paisà*, this same mechanism is resumed only periodically; throughout *Anatahan* it is *insisted upon*. In this sense, we can see something of the effect of the narrative voice and the sound track in the constitution of an apparently unified diegetic whole. In his consideration of the expository mode, Bill Nichols stretches the boundaries of the concept of diegesis from a spatio-temporal whole (which can be located primarily on the image track) to one which is more conceptual in nature, and which depends more specifically on the sound track for its ordering. In *Anatahan*, we can see how such thought can be applied to a fictional mode, in which heterogeneous diegetic planes are tied together by a metadiscourse. Moreover, the metadiscourse is aware of the heterogeneity of the narrative and functions to order it logically and to mask over cracks in the structure which, from shot to shot, sequence to sequence, threatens to fall apart at its seams. In conventional fiction film this voice remains unspoken, or is overtly tied to a particular personage within the narrative, validating the film as memory. Alternatively, the voice may be omniscient, placing the film in the function of story, explicitly 'written' by an 'author'. (This may well be the case in *Jules et Jim*, for example. The narrator appears to know the characters intimately, as the author of any fiction might, but refuses to locate himself within that fiction.) *Anatahan* places its narrative voice in a dominant position, with specific relations within the fiction, on the one hand, as a collective participant, and to the spectator on the other, by re-viewing, recalling, and retelling the narrative on our behalf. In so doing, though, the narrative voice serves mediating and controlling functions above all, for it is he who is in the privileged position within and without the fiction, and who implants a singular reading in the viewer.

In so far as the narrative is overtly rewritten, and proposes for us a singular reading, the film presents itself as an 'authored' text. It has been convenient in the past to ascribe that authorial role to Josef von Sternberg, especially considering details of his career and personality, the control he exerted over his film projects in production (he has stood as something of a tyrant over his workers), indeed over the works themselves, and, finally, over the films' viewers. Sternberg criticism has, however, chosen to mitigate this relation by putting his films on the interpretable level of poetry, or by following Sternberg's own line, citing his concern for the extremes of human emotion and their consequences. A film such as *Anatahan* however, must also be examined in terms of how it speaks to its audience. Despite Sternberg's own disappointment with the film *Anatahan* may indeed stand as an exemplar of his work. Yet what the film may point up is not insight into the human condition and human emotion, but its own tyranny.

Notes

1. From the blurb for the book *Anatahan*.
2. Yoshiro Osawa and Nagamasa Kawakita. The latter may have had a personal stake in filming the story of Anatahan, for he had been prosecuted as a B-class war criminal and had been removed from the film industry for a period of time in punishment. Joseph L. Anderson, Donald Richie, *The Japanese Film: Art and Industry* (Rutland, Vermont; Tokyo; Charles E. Tuttle, 1959), p. 163.
3. Josef von Sternberg, *Fun in a Chinese Laundry: An Autobiography* (New York; Macmillan, 1965), p. 283.
4. *Ibid.*
5. Andrew Sarris, *The American Cinema: Directors and Directions 1929–1968* (New York; E.P. Dutton, 1968), pp. 75–6.

6. John Baxter, *The Cinema of Josef von Sternberg* (London; A. Zwemmer; New York; A. S. Barnes, 1971), p. 22.
7. Raymond Durgnat, 'Six Films of Josef von Sternberg', in Bill Nichols (ed.), *Movies and Methods* (Berkeley; University of California Press, 1976), p. 273.
8. Herman G. Weinberg, *Josef von Sternberg: A Critical Study* (New York; E. P. Dutton, 1967), pp. 163–75.
9. Baxter, p. 173.
10. Andrew Sarris, *The Films of Josef von Sternberg* (New York; Museum of Modern Art, 1966).
11. See David Bordwell, 'Our Dream Cinema: Western Historiography and the Japanese Film', *Film Reader* 4 (1979), pp. 45–62.
12. Claude Ollier, 'Une aventure de la lumière', *Cahiers du Cinéma* 168 (July 1965), p. 34.
13. Weinberg, p. 163.
14. Michiro Maruyama, *Anatahan*, trans. Younghill Kang (New York; Hermitage House, 1954). Maruyama changes the names of his characters; the film retains Maruyama's pseudonyms.
15. See Herman G. Weinberg, 'Von Sternberg Films the Anatahan Story', *Sight and Sound* 22, 4 (April-June 1953), pp. 152–3.
16. Weinberg, *Josef von Sternberg*, p. 173.
17. Keiko is repeatedly called 'the Queen Bee', and the community compared to a beehive, with a number of 'drones'. These metaphors are taken from Maruyama's book.
18. Earlier in the film, it does say, 'Nothing that happens to a human being is alien to us — there but for the grace of God go I.' Even though it is singular, like the example above, this statement is set in the present tense. More an adage than a personal assertion, it is also more collective.
19. Reproduced in *Cahiers du Cinéma* 168 (July 1965), pp. 34–5.
20. See, for contemporary reports, 'White Flag Flies on Island at War', *The New York Times* (27 June 1951), p. 3; '19 More Japanese Holdouts Yield: Tell of Feuds, Killings Near Guam', *The New York Times* (1 July 1951), pp. 1, 9. The latter report contains a passage which reads like sensationalistic sales copy which would have been suitable for pitching the film:
    Theirs was the strange story of five deaths among the original thirty-three in a fight over a woman, and of feuds over who should be head man in their enforced community life.
21. I have been influenced here, and tacitly throughout this examination of narrative voice in *Anatahan* by Bill Nichols, 'Documentary Theory and Practice', *Screen* 17, 4 (Winter 1976/7), pp. 34–48. Nichols' outline specifically advances theory of the non-fiction film. Hence, while his work may not be directly applicable to the fiction film, the speculations and observations on the function of the narrator are useful in exploring films such as *Anatahan* and *Paisà*. Nichols argues that the documentary constructs its own form equivalent to, but different from, the form of narrative; significantly, these films construct a form which is equivalent to, or at least bears the markings of, documentary.
22. Ollier, p. 31.

Filmography

A. Films Directed by Josef von Sternberg

1925 **The Salvation Hunters**

Production	Academy Photoplays
Screenplay	Sternberg
Photography	Edward Gheller
Editor	Sternberg
Production Assistants	George Ruric, Robert Chapman

George K. Arthur (*The Boy*), Georgia Hale (*The Girl*), Bruce Guerin (*The Child*), Otto Matiesen (*The Man*), Nellie Bly Baker (*The Woman*), Olaf Hytten (*The Brute*), Stuart Holmes (*The Gentleman*).

Length   1808m

1926 **A Woman of the Sea**

Production	Charles Chaplin
Screenplay	Sternberg
Photography	Paul Ivano
Set Design	Danny Hall
Script Girl	Alice White
Additional Direction	Charles Chaplin

Edna Purviance, Eve Southern, Gayne Whitman.

Directed by Sternberg as *The Sea Gull*, and apparently amplified by the addition of scenes shot by Chaplin, this film was shown to the public only once before Chaplin withdrew it to his private keeping.

1926 **The Exquisite Sinner**

Production	Metro-Goldwyn-Mayer Pictures
Directors	Sternberg, Phil Rosen
Titles	Joe Farnham
Screenplay	Sternberg, Alice D. G. Miller
Story	*Escape*, a novel by Alden Brooks
Photography	Maximilian Fabian
Art Direction	Cedric Gibbons, Joseph Wright
Editor	John W. English
Assistant Director	Robert Florey
Costumes	Andre-Ani

Conrad Nagel (*Dominique Prad*), Renée Adorée (*The Gypsy Maid, Silda*), Paulette Duval (*Yvonne*), Frank Currier (*Colonel*), George K. Arthur (*His Orderly*), Matthew Betz (*The Gypsy Chief, Secchi*), Helena D'Algy, Claire Du Brey (*Dominique's Sisters*), Myrna Loy (*The Living Statue*).

Length   1822m or 1781m

Sternberg was replaced during production. In *The Cinema of Josef von Sternberg*, John Baxter says this film was also known as *Escape* and *Heaven on Earth*. The former title is that of the novel from which it was adapted. The latter title seems to be that of a re-shot and/or re-edited version of *The Exquisite Sinner* released by MGM in March 1927, credited solely to Rosen's direction.

1927 Underworld

Production	Paramount Famous Lasky Corp.
Presenters	Adolph Zukor, Jesse L. Lasky
Producer	Hector Turnbull
Screenplay	Robert N. Lee
Titles	George Marion
Adaptation	Charles Furthman
Story	Ben Hecht
Photography	Bert Glennon
Art Direction	Hans Dreier

George Bancroft (*'Bull' Weed*), Clive Brook (*'Rolls Royce'*), Evelyn Brent (*'Feathers'*), Larry Semon (*'Slippy' Lewis*), Fred Kohler (*'Buck' Mulligan*), Helen Lynch (*Mulligan's girl*), Jerry Mandy (*Paloma*), Karl Morse (*'High Collar' Sam*).

Length	2330m

1928 The Last Command

Production	Paramount Famous Lasky Corp.
Presenters	Adolph Zukor, Jesse L. Lasky
Supervisor	J. G. Bachmann
Associate Producer	B. P. Schulberg
Screenplay	John F. Goodrich
Titles	Herman J. Mankiewicz
Story	Lajos Biro
Photography	Brt Glennon
Art Direction	Hans Dreier
Editor	William Shea
Makeup	Fred C. Ryle
Technical Director	Nicholas Kobyliansky

Emil Jannings (*Grand Duke Sergius Alexander*), Evelyn Brent (*Natascha Dobrova*), William Powell (*Leo Andreiev*), Nicholas Soussanin (*Adjutant*), Michael Visaroff (*Serge, the Valet*), Jack Raymond (*Assistant Director*), Viacheslav Savitsky (*a Private*), Fritz Feld (*a Revolutionist*), Harry Semels (*Soldier Extra*), Alexander Ikonnikov, Nicholas Kobyliansky (*Drill masters*).

Length	2485m

Sternberg has claimed story-credit for this film, which was shot as *The General*, saying that it was based on an anecdote suggested by Ernst Lubitsch.

1928 The Dragnet

Production	Paramount Famous Lasky Corp.
Screenplay	Jules Furthman, Charles Furthman

Titles	Herman J. Mankiewicz
Adaptation	Jules Furthman
Story	'Nightstick' by Oliver H. P. Garrett
Photography	Harold Rosson
Art Direction	Hans Dreier
Editor	Helen Lewis

George Bancroft (*Timothy 'Two-Gun' Nolan*), Evelyn Brent (*The Magpie*), William Powell (*Dapper Frank Trent*), Fred Kohler (*Gabby Steve*), Francis McDonald (*Sniper Dawson*), Leslie Fenton (*Shakespeare Donovan*).

Length	2353m or 2398m

1928 The Docks of New York

Production	Paramount Famous Lasky Corp.
Associate Producer	J. G. Bachmann
Titles	Julian Johnson
Screenplay	Jules Furthman
Story	'The Dock Walloper' by John Monk Saunders
Photography	Harold Rosson
Art Direction	Hans Dreier
Editor	Helen Lewis

George Bancroft (*Bill Roberts*), Betty Compson (*Sadie*), Olga Baclanova (*Lou*), Clyde Cook (*Sugar Steve*), Mitchell Lewis (*Third Engineer*), Gustav von Seyffertitz (*Hymn Book Harry*), Guy Oliver (*The Crimp*), May Foster (*Mrs Crimp*), Lillian Worth (*Steve's Girl*).

Length	2195m

1929 The Case of Lena Smith

Production	Paramount Famous Lasky Corp.
Screenplay	Jules Furthman
Titles	Julian Johnson
Story	Samuel Ornitz
Photography	Harold Rosson
Art Direction	Hans Dreier, Martin Porkay
Editor	Helen Lewis

Esther Ralston (*Lena Smith*), James Hall (*Franz Hofrat*), Gustav von Seyffertitz (*Herr Hofrat*), Emily Fitzroy (*Frau Hofrat*), Fred Kohler (*Stefan*), Betty Aho (*Stefan's Sister*), Lawrence Grant (*Commissioner*), Leone Lane (*Pepi*), Kay Deslys (*Poldi*), Alex Woloshin (*Janitor*), Ann Brody (*Janitor's Wife*), Wally Albright, Jr. (*Franz, age 3*), Warner Klinger (*Franz, age 18*).

Length	2203m

1929 Thunderbolt

Production	Paramount Famous Lasky Corp.
Associate Producer	B. P. Fineman
Screenplay	Jules Furthman
Dialogue	Herman J. Mankiewicz
Titles	Joseph Mankiewicz
Story	Charles Furthman, Jules Furthman
Photography	Henry Gerrard

Art Direction	Hans Dreier
Editor	Helen Lewis
Song	'Thinkin' About My Baby', by Sam Coslow
Recording Engineer	M. M. Paggi

George Bancroft (*Thunderbolt Jim Lang*), Fay Wray (*Ritzy*), Richard Arlen (*Bob Morgan*), Tully Marshall (*Warden,*), Eugenie Besserer (*Mrs Morgan*), James Spottswood (*Snapper O'Shea*), Fred Kohler (*Bad Al Frieberg*), Robert Elliott (*Prison Chaplain*), E. H. Calvert (*District Attorney McKay*), George Irving (*Mr Corwin*), Mike Donlin (*Kentucky Sampson*), S. S. Stewart (*Negro Convict*), William L. Thorne (*Police Inspector*).

Length (silent version)   2228m
Running Time (Movietone sound version) 95 min.

1930 **Der Blaue Engel/The Blue Angel**

Production	Ufa/Paramount
Producer	Erich Pommer
Screenplay	Carl Zuckmayer, Karl Vollmöller, and Robert Liebmann
Story	*Professor Unrat* by Heinrich Mann
Photography	Günther Rittau, Hans Schneeberger
Art Direction	Otto Hunte, Emil Hasler
Sound Engineer	Fritz Thiery
Editors	S. K. Winston (English version)
	Walter Klee (German version)
Songs	'Ich bin von Kopf bis Fuss aus Liebe Eingestellt'/'Falling in Love Again', 'Ich bin die fesche Lola'/'They Call Me Naughty Lola', 'Nimm Dich in Acht vor blonden Frauen'/'Beware Blonde Women', 'Kinder, heut' Abend such' ich mich was aus'/'I Gotta Get A Man': music by Friedrich Holländer; German lyrics by Robert Liebmann; English lyrics by Sam Winston
Music	Friedrich Holländer

Emil Jannings (*Professor Immanuel Rath*), Marlene Dietrich (*Lola Lola*), Kurt Gerron (*Kiepert*), Rosa Valetti (*Guste*), Hans Albers (*Mazeppa*), Reinhold Bernt (*Clown*), Eduard von Winterstein (*Headmaster*), Rolf Müller (*Angst*), Roland Verno (*Lohmann*), Karl Bollhaus (*Ertzum*), Robert Klein-Lork (*Goldstaub*), Karl Huszar-Puffy (*Proprietor*), Wilhelm Diegelmann (*Sea Captain*), Gerhard Bienert (*Policeman*), Ilse Furstenberg (*Maid*), Hans Roth (*Caretaker*).

Running Time	109 min.

1930 **Morocco**

Production	Paramount Publix Corp.
Producer	Hector Turnbull
Screenplay	Jules Furthman
Story	*Amy Jolly* by Benno Vigny
Photography	Lee Garmes
Additional Photography	Lucien Ballard
Art Direction	Hans Dreier
Songs:	'Give Me the Man',
	'What Am I Bid For My Apples?'
	music by Karl Hajos; lyrics by
	Leo Robin. 'Quand l'Amour Meurt'
	by Millandy and Cremieux

Gary Cooper (*Legionnaire Tom Brown*), Marlene Dietrich (*Amy Jolly*), Adolph Menjou (*La Bessière*), Ullrich Haupt (*Adjutant Caesar*), Eve Southern (*Mme Caesar*), Francis McDonald (*Sergeant*), Paul Porcasi (*Lo Tinto*), Juliette Compton (*Anna Dolores*), Albert Conti (*Colonel Quinnevieres*), Emile Chautard (*General*).

Running Time	90 min.

1931 **Dishonored**

Production	Paramount Publix Corp.
Screenplay	Daniel N. Rubin
Story	'X 27' by Sternberg
Photography	Lee Garmes
Art Direction	Hans Dreier
Sound Engineer	Harry D. Mills

Marlene Dietrich (*X 27*), Victor McLaglen (*Lieutenant Kranau*), Lew Cody (*Colonel Kovrin*), Gustav von Seyffertitz (*Head of Secret Service*), Warner Oland (*General von Hindau*), Barry Norton (*Young Lieutenant*), Davison Clark (*Court Officer*), Wilfred Lucas (*General Dymov*).

Running Time	91 min.

1931 **An American Tragedy**

Production	Paramount Publix Corp.
Screenplay	Sternberg, Samuel Hoffenstein
Story	*An American Tragedy*, a novel by Theodore Dreiser
Photography	Lee Garmes
Art Direction	Hans Dreier
Sound Engineer	Harry D. Mills

Phillips Holmes (*Clyde Griffiths*), Sylvia Sidney (*Roberta Alden*), Frances Dee (*Sondra Finchley*), Irving Pichel (*Orville Mason*), Frederick Burton (*Samuel Griffiths*), Claire McDowell (*Mrs Samuel Griffiths*), Wallace Middleton (*Gilbert Griffiths*), Vivian Winston (*Myra Griffiths*), Emmett Corrigan (*Bellcap*), Lucille La Verne (*Mrs Asa Griffiths*), Charles B. Middleton (*Jephson*), Albert Hart (*Titus Alden*), Fanny Midgely (*Mrs

Alden), Arline Judge (*Bella Griffiths*), Evelyn Pierce (*Bertine Cranston*), Arnold Korff (*Judge*), Elizabeth Forrester (*Jill Trumbell*), Russell Powell (*Coroner Fred Heit*), Imboden Parrish (*Earl Newcomb*), Richard Kramer (*Deputy Sheriff Kraut*).

Running Time   95 min.

1932 Shanghai Express

Production	Paramount Publix Corp.
Producer	Adolph Zukor
Screenplay	Jules Furthman
Story	Harry Hervey
Photography	Lee Garmes
Art Direction	Hans Dreier
Costumes	Travis Banton

Marlene Dietrich (*Shanghai Lily*), Clive Brook (*Donald Harvey*), Anna May Wong (*Hui Fei*), Warner Oland (*Henry Chang*), Eugene Pallette (*Sam Salt*), Lawrence Grant (*Rev. Carmichael*), Louise Closser Hale (*Mrs Haggerty*), Gustav von Seyffertitz (*Baum*), Emile Chautard (*Major Lenard*).

Running Time   80 min.

1932 Blonde Venus

Production	Paramount Publix Corp.
Producer	Sternberg
Screenplay	Jules Furthman, S. K. Lauren
Story	Sternberg
Photography	Bert Glennon
Art Direction	Wiard Ihnen
Songs	'Hot Voodoo', 'You Little So and So': music by Sam Coslow, lyrics by Ralph Rainger; 'I Couldn't Be Annoyed': music by Leo Robin, lyrics by Dick Whiting

Marlene Dietrich (*Helen Faraday*), Herbert Marshall (*Ned Faraday*), Cary Grant (*Nick Townsend*), Dickie Moore (*Johnny Faraday*), Gene Morgan (*Ben Smith*), Rita La Roy ('*Taxi Belle' Hooper*), Robert Emmett (*Dan O'Connor*), Sidney Toler (*Detective Wilson*), Morgan Wallace (*Dr. Pierce*), Cecil Cunningham (*Nightclub Hostess*).

Running Time   80 min.

1934 The Scarlet Empress

Production	Paramount Productions Inc.
Producer	Adolph Zukor
Screenplay	Manuel Komroff, adapted from a diary of Catherine the Great
Photography	Bert Glennon
Art Direction	Hans Dreier
Icons and Paintings	Richard Kollorsz
Sculpture	Peter Ballbusch
Titles and Effects	Gordon Jennings

Music	John Leopold, W. Frank Harling, from themes by Tchaikovsky (Fourth Symphony, *Marche Slave*, '1812' Overture), Mendelssohn (*Rondo Capriccioso, Midsummer Night's Dream*), Wagner (*The Ride of The Walküre*)
Additional Music	Sternberg
Costumes	Travis Banton

Marlene Dietrich (*Sophia Frederica, later Catherine II*), John Lodge (*Count Alexei*), Sam Jaffe (*Grand Duke Peter*), Louise Dresser (*Empress Elizabeth*), Maria Sieber (*Sophia Frederica as a Child*), C. Aubrey Smith (*Prince August*), Olive Tell (*Princess Johanna*), Ruthelma Stevens (*Countess Elizabeth*), Gavin Gordon (*Gregory Orloff*), Jameson Thomas (*Lieutenant Ovtsyn*), Hans von Twardowski (*Ian Shuvolov*), Davison Clark (*Simeon Tevedovsky, Archimandrite and Archbishop*), Erville Alderson (*Chancellor*), Gerald Fielding (*Lieutenant Dimitri*).

Running Time	105 min.

1935 **The Devil is a Woman**

Production	Paramount Productions Inc.
Screenplay	John Dos Passos, S. K. Winston
Story	*La Femme et le pantin*, by Pierre Louys
Photography	Sternberg
Assistant Photographer	Lucien Ballard
Art Direction	Hans Dreier
Costumes	Travis Banton
Music	Ralph Rainger, Andres Setaro, based on themes from *Caprice Espagnole* by Rimsky-Korsakoff
Song	'Three Sweethearts Have I': music by Ralph Rainger, lyrics by Leo Robin
Editor	Sam Winston

Marlene Dietrich (*Concha Perez*), Lionel Atwill (*Don Pascal*), Cesar Romero (*Antonio Galvan*), Edward Everett Horton (*Don Paquito*), Alison Skipworth (*Senora Perez*), Don Alvarado (*Morenito*), Morgan Wallace (*Dr. Mendez*), Tempe Pigott (*Tuerta*), Jill Dennett (*Maria*), Lawrence Grant (*Conductor*), Charles Sellon (*Letter Writer*), Luisa Espinal (*Gypsy Dancer*), Hank Mann (*Foreman, Snowbound Train*), Edwin Maxwell (*Superintendent, Cigarette Factory*).

Running Time	85 min.

1935 **Crime and Punishment**

Production	Columbia Pictures
Producer	B. P. Schulberg
Screenplay	S. K. Lauren, Joseph Anthony, from Dostoyevsky's novel
Photography	Lucien Ballard
Art Direction	Stephen Gooson

Costumes	Murray Mayer
Music	Louis Silvers
Editor	Richard Cahoon

Peter Lorre *(Raskolnikov)*, Edward Arnold *(Inspector Porfiry)*, Marian Marsh *(Sonya)*, Tala Birell *(Antonya)*, Elizabeth Risdon *(Raskolnikov's Mother)*, Robert Allen *(Dmitri)*, Douglass Dumbrille *(Grilov)*, Gene Lockhart *(Lushin)*, Charles Waldron *(Rector of the University)*, Thurston Hall *(Editor)*, Johnny Arthur *(Clerk)*, Mrs Patrick Campbell *(Pawnbroker)*, Rafaela Ottiano *(Landlady)*, Michael Mark *(Painter Prisoner)*.

Running Time	89 min.

1936 **The King Steps Out**

Production	Columbia Pictures
Producer	William Perlberg
Screenplay	Sidney Buchman
Story	*Sissi*, an operetta by Ernst and Herbert Marischka after the play by Ernest Decsey and Gustav Hohn
Photography	Lucien Ballard
Art Direction	Stephen Gooson
Costumes	Ernst Dryden
Choreography	Albertina Rasch
Music	Fritz Kreisler
Arrangements	Howard Jackson
Songs	'Stars In My Eyes', 'Madly in Love', 'Learn How to Lose', 'What Shall Remain?': music by Fritz Kreisler, lyrics by Dorothy Fields
Vocal Conductor	Josef A. Pasternack
Assistant Director	Wilhelm Thiele
Editor	Viola Lawrence

Grace Moore *(Sissi)*, Franchot Tone *(Franz Josef)*, Walter Connolly *(Maximilian)*, Raymond Walburn *(Von Kempen)*, Victor Jory *(Palfi)*, Elizabeth Risdon *(Sofia)*, Nana Bryant *(Louise)*, Frieda Inescort *(Helena)*, Thurston Hall *(Major)*, Herman Bing *(Pretzelberger)*, George Hassell *(Herlicka)*, John Arthur *(Chief of Secret Police)*.

Running Time	85 min.

1937 **I, Claudius** (unfinished)

Production	Alexander Korda for London Films
Screenplay	Lajos Biro, Carl Zuckmayer
Additional Material	Lester Cohen
Story	*I, Claudius* and *Claudius the God* by Robert Graves
Photography	Georges Perinal
Art Direction	Vincent Korda

Costumes   John Armstrong
Choreography   Agnes De Mille
Charles Laughton (*Tiberius Claudius Drusus*), Merle Oberon (*Messalina*), Flora Robson (*Livia*), Emlyn Williams (*Caligula*), Robert Newton (*Centurion*), John Clements (*Valens*).

1939 Sergeant Madden

Production	Metro-Goldwyn-Mayer
Producer	J. Walter Ruben
Screenplay	Wells Root
Story	'A Gun in His Hand' by William A. Ullman
Photography	John Seitz
Art Direction	Cedric Gibbons, Randall Duel
Montage	Peter Ballbusch
Music	William Axt
Editor	Conrad A. Nervig

Wallace Beery (*Sean Madden*), Tom Brown (*Al Boylan, Jr.*), Alan Curtis (*Dennis Madden*), Laraine Day (*Eileen Daly*), Fay Holden (*Mary Madden*), Marc Lawrence (*'Piggy' Ceders*), Marian Martin (*Charlotte*), David Gorcey (*'Punchy'*).

Running Time   82 min.

1942 The Shanghai Gesture

Production	Arnold Pressburger for United Artists
Associate Producer	Albert de Courville
Screenplay	Sternberg, Karl Vollmöller, Geza Herczeg, Jules Furthman
Story	*The Shanghai Gesture,* a play by John Colton
Photography	Paul Ivano
Art Direction	Boris Leven
Set Decorator	Howard Bristol
Murals	Keye Luke
Costumes	Royer, Oleg Cassini
Wigs	Hazel Rogers
Music	Richard Hageman
Editor	Sam Winston

Gene Tierney (*'Poppy'*), Ona Munson (*'Mother' Gin Sling*), Walter Huston (*Sir Guy Charteris*), Victor Mature (*'Doctor' Omar*), Phyllis Brooks (*Dixie Pomeroy*), Albert Bassermann (*Commissioner*), Clyde Fillmore (*Comprador*), Eric Blore (*Bookkeeper*), Ivan Lebedeff (*Gambler*), Marcel Dalio (*Croupier*), Mikhail Rasumny (*Cashier*), Michael Delmatoff (*Barkeeper*), Maria Ouspenskaya (*Amah*), Mike Mazurki (*Coolie*), Rex Evans (*Counsellor Brooks*), John Abbott (*Escort*).

Running Time   98 min.

1944 **The Town**

Production	United States Office of War Information
Producer	Phillip Dunne
Screenplay	Josef Krumgold
Photography	Larry Madison
Running Time	12 min.

1951 **Jet Pilot**

Production	Howard Hughes Productions/RKO Teleradio Pictures/Universal-International
Producer	Jules Furthman
Screenplay	Jules Furthman
Photography	Winton C. Hoch (Technicolor)
Aerial Photography	Philip C. Cochran
Art Direction	Albert S. D'Agostino, Field Gray
Set Decoration	Darrell Silvera, Harley Miller
Costumes	Michael Woulfe
Music	Bronislau Kaper
Musical Direction	C. Bakaleinikoff
Editors	Michael R. McAdam, Marry Marker, William M. Moore
Editorial Supervision	James Wilkinson

John Wayne (*Col. Jim Shannon*), Janet Leigh (*Lieut. Anna Orlieff*), Jay C. Flippen (*Major-General Black*), Paul Fix (*Major Rexford*), Richard Rober (*George Rivers*), Roland Winters (*Col. Sokolov*), Hans Conried (*Col. Matoff*), Ivan Triesault (*Gen. Langrad*), John Bishop (*Major Sinclair*), Perdita Chandler (*Georgia Rexford*), Joyce Compton (*Mrs Simpson*), Denver Pyle (*Mr Simpson*).

Running Time	112 min.

1952 **Macao**

Production	RKO Radio Pictures
Producer	Alex Gottlieb
Additional Direction	Nicholas Ray
Screenplay	Bernard C. Schoenfeld, Stanley Rubin
Story	Bob Williams
Photography	Harry J. Wild
Art Direction	Albert S. D'Agostino, Ralph Berger
Set Decoration	Darrell Silvera, Harley Miller
Costumes	Michael Woulfe
Music	Anthony Collins
Musical Direction	C. Bakaleinikoff
Songs	'One For My Baby' by Johnny Mercer and Harold Arlen; 'Ocean Breeze', 'You Kill Me' by Jules Styne and Leo Robin
Editors	Samuel E. Beetley, Robert Golden

Robert Mitchum (*Nick Cochran*), Jane Russell (*Julie Benson*), Gloria Grahame (*Margie*), William Bendix (*Lawrence Trumble*), Thomas Gomez

(*Lieutenant Sebastian*), Brad Dexter (*Halloran*), Edward Ashley (*Martin Stewart*), Philip Ahn (*Itzumi*), Vladimir Sokolov (*Kwan Sum Tang*), Don Zelaya ('*Gimpy*').
Running Time   81 min.

1953 The Saga of Anatahan

Production	Daiwa Productions-Towa/ Pathé-Contemporary
Producers	Yoshio Osawa, Nagamasa Kawakita, Sternberg
Associate Producer	Takimura
Screenplay	Sternberg
Story	*Anatahan* by Michiro Maruyama, and an article in *Life* magazine
Japanese Dialogue	Asano
Photography	Sternberg, Okazaki
Art Direction	Kono
Artist	Watanabe
Music	Akira Ifukube
Special Assistant	Okawa
Assistant Director	Taguchi
Editor	Miyata

Akemi Negishi ('*Queen Bee*'), Tadashi Suganuma ('*Husband*'), Kisaburo Sawamura, Shoji Nakayama, Jun Fujikawa, Hiroshi Kondo, Shozo Miyashita (*the 'Drones'*), Tsuruemon Bando, Kikuji Onoe (*the 'Skippers'*), Rokuriro Kineya (*Maruyama, the samisen-player*), Daijiro Tamura, Takashi Kitagawa, Takeshi Suzuki (*the 'Homesick Ones'*), Shiro Amikura (*the 'Patriot'*).
Running Time   92 min.

B. Other Film Work

1919 The Mystery of the Yellow Room

Production	Realart
Director	Emile Chautard

(Sternberg claims to have worked on this film.)

1920 The Highest Bidder

Production	Goldwyn Pictures
Director	Wallace Worsley
Assistant Director	Jo Sternberg

1922 The Bohemian Girl (UK)

Production	Alliance Productions
Director	Harley Knoles

(In *The Cinema of Josef von Sternberg*, John Baxter claims that Sternberg was assistant director on this film.)

1923 **By Divine Right**

Production	Grand-Asher Distributing Corp.
Director	R. William Neill
Screenplay	Josef von Sternberg

1924 **Vanity's Price**

Production	Gothic Pictures
Director	R. William Neill
Assistant Director	Josef von Sternberg

1925 **The Masked Bride**

Production	Metro-Golwyn-Mayer
Director	Christy Cabanne
Additional Direction	Josef von Sternberg

(Sternberg began directing this film, which was completed by Cabanne.)

1927 **Children of Divorce**

Production	Famous Players-Lasky
Director	Frank Lloyd
Additional Direction	Josef von Sternberg

1927 **It**

Production	Famous Players-Lasky
Director	Clarence Badger
Additional Direction	Josef von Sternberg

1928 **The Street of Sin**

Production	Paramount Famous Lasky Corp.
Director	Mauritz Stiller
Story	Josef von Sternberg

1928 **The Wedding March**

Production	Paramount Famous Lasky Corp.
Director	Erich von Stroheim

(Sternberg apparently edited the film with Stroheim's approval; uncredited.)

1938 **The Great Waltz**

Production	Metro-Goldwyn-Mayer
Director	Julien Duvivier
Additional Direction	Josef von Sternberg

1938 **I Take This Woman**

Production	Metro-Goldwyn-Mayer
Director	W. S. Van Dyke

(Sternberg began to direct this film as *New York Cinderella,* was replaced by Frank Borzage, and the latter eventually by Van Dyke.)

1946 **Duel in the Sun**

Production	Selznick Productions
Director	King Vidor
Assistant Director	Josef von Sternberg

Some Selected Reading

Sternberg's consistently astonishing book of recollections and opinion, *Fun in a Chinese Laundry* (London; Secker and Warburg, 1966/New York; Macmillan, 1965) is a crucial work, but needs a symptomatic reading, treading warily round the persona dominating each of its pages. Herman Weinberg's homage to the director, *Josef von Sternberg* (New York; E. P. Dutton and Co., Inc., 1967), has recently been reprinted in facsimile by the Arno Press of New York, while John Baxter's *The Cinema of Josef von Sternberg* is still in print in the US (New York; A. S. Barnes). *The Films of Josef von Sternberg* by Andrew Sarris (New York; The Museum of Modern Art, 1966) is out of print, but valuable for the quality of Sarris' comments on individual films.

The 'scripts' of *The Blue Angel*, and of *Morocco* and *Shanghai Express*, are published by Lorrimer in London, and Simon & Schuster in New York. The former is a translation of the German-language version of the film, introduced by Sternberg: it is rather different from the English-language version which was made concurrently with it, and which is the version regularly circulated in the UK.

Productive critical work on particular films is rare. Robin Wood's 'The Play of Light and Shade: *The Scarlet Empress*', in *Personal Views: Explorations in Film* (London; Gordon Fraser, 1976), is perhaps the most stimulating to have been published in the last decade or so. In a later article on *Blonde Venus*, 'Venus de Marlene', *Film Comment*, Vol. 14, No. 2 (March-April 1978), pp. 58-63, Wood takes issue with Laura Mulvey's very influential and important essay on the fetishisation of images of women in the cinema, 'Visual Pleasure and Narrative Cinema', *Screen*, Vol. 16, No. 3 (Autumn 1975), pp. 6-18. One might read in relation to both these texts Bill Nichols' extremely detailed reading of the film's elaboration and control of the Dietrich image, *'Blonde Venus*: Playing with Performance', in *Ideology and the Image* (Bloomington and London; Indiana University Press, 1980). See also my own 'On the Naked Thighs of Miss Dietrich', *Wide Angle*, Vol. 2, No. 2 (Spring 1978), pp. 18-25.

In French, *Cahiers du Cinéma*, No. 168 (July 1965), in a special section on Sternberg includes Claude Ollier's 'Une aventure de la lumière', pp. 28-36, an analysis of *Anatahan*.

UK 16mm Availability List of Films
Directed by Josef von Sternberg

The Salvation Hunters	Cinegate
Thunderbolt	Rank Film Library
The Blue Angel	British Film Institute
	(Cinegate from 1981)
Morocco	British Film Institute
Dishonored	British Film Institute
An American Tragedy	Rank Film Library
Shanghai Express	British Film Institute
Blonde Venus	British Film Institute
The Scarlet Empress	Rank Film Library
The Devil is a Woman	British Film Institute
Crime and Punishment	Columbia-EMI-Warner
The Shanghai Gesture	Cinegate
The Town	British Film Institute
Jet Pilot	British Film Institute
Macao	Harris/Films
The Saga of Anatahan	British Film Institute

A documentary on the abandoned Claudius project is available:
The Epic that Never Was   London Film Productions

Distributors' Addresses

British Film Institute
Distribution Library
81 Dean Street
London W1V 6AA
(01) 734 6451

Cinegate
Gate Cinema
87 Notting Hill Gate
London W11
(01) 727 2651

Columbia-EMI-Warner
16mm Division
135 Wardour Street
London W1
(01) 439 7621

Harris/Films
Glenbuck House
Glenbuck Road
Surbiton
Surrey
(01) 399 0022

London Film Productions
6 Goodwin's Court
St Martin's Lane
London WC2N 4LL
(062 84) 5919 (NB: this is the correct phone
number, though it's not a London one.)

Rank Film Library
PO Box 20
Great West Road
Brentford
Middlesex
(01) 560 0762